The Turning of the Seasons

Tales of a smallholding life

Mary-Jane Houlton

Paperback edition, published 2022

Copyright © Mary-Jane Houlton, 2022

All rights reserved. No part of this book may be reproduced, stored in a retrieval system, stored in a database or transmitted in any form or by any means, electronic, mechanical, photocopying, recording or otherwise without the prior written permission of the author.

This book is a memoir. It reflects the author's recollections of experiences over time. Any opinions expressed within this book are the author's personal opinions and do not reflect those of any other person or organisation.

All URLs correct at the time of writing.

Book cover design by ebooklaunch.com

Other books by the author

Just Passing Through – A nomadic life afloat in France
A Simple Life – Living off-grid in a wooden cabin in France

Contents

Preface 9
Introduction 13
Part 1 – The early years 21
Chapter 1: The smallholding bug 23
Chapter 2: The turning of the seasons 31
Chapter 3: Chicken addiction 36
Chapter 4: Oh, for a crystal ball 47
Chapter 5: Ram 55
Chapter 6: Loss 65
Chapter 7: One door closes, another opens 71
Chapter 8: Is it the winning that counts, or the taking part? 85
Chapter 9: Full circle 96
Chapter 10: Grow your own 104
Chapter 11: Wedding 112
Part 2 – Settling in 121
Chapter 12: New faces 123
Chapter 13: Getting along with pigs 132
Chapter 14: A step too far 139
Chapter 15: A bad year 147
Chapter 16: Understanding donkeys 165
Chapter 17: From pig to pork 174
Chapter 18: Orphan 182
Chapter 19: Ain't got no roots 188

Chapter 20: Jack Frost 194

Part 3 – The letting go **199**

Chapter 21: Transitions 201

Chapter 22: Ladies that lunch 206

Chapter 23: Paradise lost part 1 212

Chapter 24: Making a difference 216

Chapter 25: Paradise lost part 2 221

Chapter 26: Saying goodbye 226

Chapter 27: How did *that* happen? 236

Part 4 – Moving on **247**

Chapter 28: Finding *Olivia Rose* 249

Chapter 29: What now? 256

Chapter 30: The adventure begins 264

Acknowledgements 268

About the author 269

Excerpt from *Just Passing Through* 271

Preface

For thirteen years, from 2004 to 2017, my husband Michael and I lived in Wales. During that time we had a smallholding where we learnt how to look after a small flock of Jacob sheep, some Royal Berkshire pigs, a collection of hens that went up and down in number on the whim of the local foxes, an Icelandic horse and a donkey. With no experience to guide us our learning curve was a steep one but those heart-warming, sometimes heart-breaking, years taught me so much more than the practical realities of animal husbandry.

I experienced the joy of watching a new life come into the world, a lamb nudging against its mother for milk, or a donkey foal teetering on gangly legs. I suffered as my animals lost their lives: hens butchered by a fox, a lamb or a ewe lost to so many possible causes, not least my own ignorance in the early days which was a hard thing to bear and to take responsibility for. As we intended to eat our own meat I had to adjust my mindset, sanitised by so many years of supermarket shopping, and accept that it was one thing to pick up a packet of chicken legs from a chiller cabinet and quite another to kill and pluck a chicken that I had raised from birth.

Those smallholding years weren't just about the animals, they were also about people and becoming part of a community. We were surrounded by other smallholders, as well as mainstream farmers, most of whom knew a great deal more than we did, and who were incredibly generous and kind with both their time and their knowledge.

This book follows us as we searched for a life that felt really worth the living. It's not written as a diary, a sequential day-by-day account, nor as a detailed blueprint of how to be a smallholder, but more as a memoir, an amalgamation of our experiences, moving from the early years of learning to the middle years of consolidation as each passing season added to what we learnt in the last one, and finally to the letting go, as we left in search of a new challenge and a very different life.

We spent much of our time on this journey asking questions, some of them the nuts and bolts queries that are inevitable when you've thrown yourself in at the deep end and have no idea what you're doing. Other questions were more philosophical. How would it feel to eat an animal that we helped bring into the world, or indeed to kill it by our own hand? Were our efforts to live a sustainable life making any difference or was it a pointless waste of time? Was it wrong to pursue happiness above all other goals?

By the time we reached the end of this phase in our lives I was fifty-seven years old, Michael was fifty, and we were different people to those you meet in the first pages of this book. It felt as if we might finally have acquired a little wisdom, a greater understanding of our world and what we wanted from it. As the seasons inexorably turn and move on, so did we also feel that urge to move on, to exchange the steady, wonderful life we had made for ourselves and replace it with something completely different, a step into the unknown. It is possible to love a place and a lifestyle dearly, to treasure the personal connections of family and friends, but also to acknowledge that leaving it behind is the right thing to do.

This book is the prequel to *Just Passing Through*, my first book and one that was part memoir, part travelogue, an account of a journey cruising through European waters. *The Turning of the Seasons* provides an insight into how we fell in love with a different way of living, a time when we were settled, closely connected to our Welsh hills and our beloved animals, and it also explains why we left it all behind to live a nomadic life on a boat. I hope you enjoy it.

Mary-Jane Houlton

Introduction

A day in the life

The lamb lay on its side in the grass. It was barely a day old, its skin loose and wrinkled like a jumper that was a couple of sizes too big. This didn't concern me because they often seemed to grow into their skin and fill it out once they had a few days' milk inside them, but it struggled to lift its head as I approached and this did worry me.

The lamb's mother, Morag, stood a few paces off, staring at me balefully while her other two newborn lambs headbutted her teats for milk, oblivious to the fact that their sibling might be failing. She swung around, almost knocking her babies over, trotted away a few paces and then back again, her anxiety and hostility evident. She was the wildest of our Jacob sheep and always kept her distance, never at ease in my company. She was an experienced and capable mother, and having triplets was not usually a problem for her. Somehow they all managed to get enough milk, although the smallest and weakest always stayed that way, never first in line at feeding time.

I came closer and ran my hand gently over the lamb. It was still warm, but its breathing was laboured. I shot an apologetic look at Morag and picked it up, tucking it down inside my coat, and then headed back home.

Michael was standing at the cooker as I walked in. There were sausages and bacon under the grill and baked beans bubbled gently in a saucepan.

'Where have you been?' he asked, cracking two fresh eggs into the frying pan. 'Breakfast is almost ready.'

'Complications,' I said, struggling to get out of my coat and fend off two curious dogs without dropping the lamb.

He turned around. 'Oh. Who does that belong to?'

'One of Morag's. It was fine last night.' I popped the lamb into a cardboard box that always sat next to the Rayburn during lambing time and then ran upstairs. I pulled off my dirty sheep clothes, leaving them in a pile on the floor, threw on something cleaner and ran back down the stairs again. Two plates full of a hearty breakfast awaited me on the kitchen work surface. Unfortunately, they weren't for us. I scooped them up and opened the door.

'Can you get some powdered milk on the hob?' I said on my

way out. 'I'm hoping that a good feed will be enough to get that lamb back on its feet.'

Michael nodded.

On the far side of our patio was The Studio, a self-contained annexe that we had converted into a B&B. This breakfast was for our guests but I could hear my stomach rumbling in protest as I walked over. I'd spent longer with the sheep than expected and hadn't had time for my own breakfast. Some mornings I would linger with our guests, talking about the animals and life in the village, but today wasn't one of those days. I needed to get some milk down that lamb, some breakfast down me, and then do yet another costume change to go to work.

We ran our own business, which thankfully meant we could be flexible in the way we arranged our day. When we first moved into the village together we had a garden design and landscaping business. I had started this up by myself fifteen years ago, and when I met Michael he then joined me, but the hard physical work had taken its toll, and I struggled with back problems and arthritis. As a result we had moved in a new direction, a carpet cleaning and stone floor restoration business, which supposedly was less physically demanding, although the jury was still out on that one. One business was fading, the other growing, which left us still doing a bit of both. Today was a carpet cleaning day, a one-room job which wouldn't take long, just as well as I knew I would be fretting about the lamb as soon as I left the house. In our early days Michael would have gone out to work alone if a lamb was poorly like this, leaving me behind to look after it. However, time had taught us that watching a sick animal was often akin to watching paint dry and that, unless the problem was very serious, it was better to get on with something productive and give the animal time to rest.

An hour later the lamb had managed a decent feed of a powdered milk substitute and was already looking better, the guests had paid up and would leave when they were ready, and we were loading up the van with the carpet cleaning kit, heading off to a holiday cottage in the middle of nowhere.

We lived in the Brecon Beacons in Wales and most of our work was in the tourist industry, a mixture of hotels, cottages, and B&Bs similar to ourselves. It was our own B&B that first gave us the idea to try our hand at this business, one of those strange quirks of life where you go off at a completely unexpected tangent. We needed the carpets cleaned in The Studio and whilst we were waiting for someone to visit and give us a quote Michael had the idea that it was something that we could do. And so we did. We attended the necessary training courses, bought the kit, had the van signwritten with a new logo and hoped that the business would slowly build up. Working at both the B&B and carpet cleaning brought in just enough of an income to keep our heads above water and allow us to manage the smallholding, which was never going to be a profitable affair.

We were back home a few hours later, both of us wondering what we would find as we opened the kitchen door. The lamb had its head up and was looking much perkier than when we left. I picked it up, its body warm, its little heart beating strong under my hands, and watched the smile spread across Michael's face, knowing it was mirrored on my own.

'Time to take this little fellow back to his grumpy mum,' I said.

Morag's head came up as soon as I walked into the field and she watched me intently as I headed towards her. I held the lamb out in front of me so that she could see it, stopped a short distance away and put it down gently on the grass. This was the tricky bit. I had known lambs panic and run off in the opposite direction or try and latch onto another ewe, which usually ended up with them being seen off, or the rightful mother deciding that she no longer accepted the lamb as it had been away for too long. Morag stared at it for a second, then whickered quietly. The lamb tottered off towards her and after a few false starts eventually found the teat and started sucking noisily. I breathed a sigh of relief and left them to it. I would need to keep an eye on it, but hopefully it was on the right track now.

The dogs had been waiting patiently at the gate, knowing that their evening walk was next. We all loved this time of the day. I walked through the village, past the pub, over the main road, cut across the field and up a dead-end single-track lane.

From here I turned up one of the ancient drover's tracks that crisscrossed this part of the country and finally up onto the hill. Jessie, my old Labrador-collie cross was thirteen years old now, and took her time. Lucy, our young collie, was off in the distance, a flash of black and white streaking through the bracken.

I circled round on the spine of the hill until I was looking down on our home, and the little patches of land that we rented for our smallholding. Behind our cottage the slopes of the Black Mountains rose steeply from the valley floor. I sat down on the grass, as I so often did, and watched the early evening sunlight run its fingers down the hill. Jessie sat by my side and I stroked her soft head, a habit so ingrained I was unaware I was doing it. Lucy whined softly. She didn't approve of stopping, but when I ignored her she took herself off to explore further along the track.

That was my life down there and seeing it from my vantage point on high always gave me a sense of wonder. After very humble beginnings, just two Jacob ewes purchased in a hurry and in total ignorance of what constitutes a sound animal, we now had a thriving flock of sixteen ewes and lambs, as well as pigs and hens. After four years we were beginning to feel more comfortable with what we were doing, slightly less panic-stricken when something went wrong. It had been a precipitous learning curve and I envied those who were born into a farming family, learning from their parents and their grandparents and hopefully avoiding some of the mistakes that we made along the way. The difficult times were far outweighed by the good, and I felt incredibly lucky that we had found this life – or perhaps it had found us.

Lucy returned, panting from her explorations, her tongue lolling out of her mouth. She stuck her nose in my face and then trotted off a few steps, before turning to wait for me. Her message was clear. I'd had my chance to sit and think, and she was ready to go on. Fair enough. It was time for dinner.

Mary-Jane Houlton

Part 1

The early years

Mary-Jane Houlton

Chapter 1

The smallholding bug

Why do people become smallholders? Is it because of some romantic notion that they can live 'a good life', one that is more fulfilling and less stressful? Does it stem from an urge to live sustainably and do their bit for the planet, or perhaps to rescue animals from the horrors of industrial farming practices? Or is it a response to some instinctive urge to spend our days outside in the open air, in tune with the natural world around us, rather than being confined in cars and offices?

I suspect for many people it is a combination of all those things. It certainly was for us. An experienced smallholder would raise a cynical eyebrow at the notion that there was anything romantic about dealing with a fly-struck sheep riddled with maggots, but life would be sad and dull without dreams to inspire us. If our idea of paradise becomes tempered by reality over time, then it's not the end of the world, just an adjustment, a different way of looking at things.

Neither of us had any knowledge of how to run a smallholding. Michael had spent the first nineteen years of his working life at sea, beginning as a cadet in the RFA, the Royal Fleet Auxiliary. He gained his Master Mariner Certificate and, after ten years working on the supply ships for the Royal Navy, left the RFA to work as a Navigation Officer for P&O cruise liners. These huge ships carried 2,700 passengers and 1,400 crew and his travels would take him around the Caribbean, the Mediterranean, the Americas and the Far East.

By the time I met him he had downsized to smaller boats, working for Trinity House, the organisation responsible for maintaining the lighthouses and lightvessels around England and Wales. When I first asked him what he did for a living, he simply said he changed lightbulbs. Big ones.

I had begun my working life as a marketing executive, moving restlessly from one multinational company to another. I spent between two to three hours of every day commuting to a desk surrounded on three sides by screens, one of many in an open plan office. My time was measured by the number of meetings I attended in any one day, the number of telephone calls I made or the number of reports I wrote. Occasionally I would change the routine and fly to Europe or the States, but a new time zone didn't change the content of the day: more meetings, more presentations in an identical office block, all concrete and darkened windows, and then it was a taxi ride back to the airport. That drive was often all I ever saw of the country I had travelled to.

The working days were long and the weekends short. Sunday night would roll around all too quickly and with it came an insidious sense of dread at climbing back on the merry-go-round again. Life felt as if it was moving too fast, out of my control. Time was money in a capitalist society and there was an unspoken pressure not to waste it or lose track of it. I wasn't alone in living this type of life. I was part of the system so in some ways it felt perfectly normal. But as the years flew by it began to feel ever more pointless, a terrible waste, and eventually there came a Monday morning when I didn't climb back on the merry-go-round. I left that world and started up my own business in garden design and landscaping, hoping that in working for myself I could find a good reason to get up in the morning again as well as regaining control over how I spent my days.

At this point I met Michael and we had both known almost immediately that we wanted to spend the rest of our lives together. He left the sea, retrained in hard landscaping and joined me in the business. We had sold our respective terraced cottages and bought a bigger cottage in the village where Michael already lived. He had his Icelandic horse, Snari, kept at livery in a local yard due to the fact that he had, until he met me, spent half his life away at sea. I had my two dogs and three cats, but that was the sum total of our knowledge of the animal world and it was of no use whatsoever.

We had put the word around that we were looking for a bit of land to rent, expecting that it would take years for it to materialise as we were incomers and the local land-owning families who had been born in the village would bide their time, getting to know us before giving up any of their precious land. We thought we had plenty of time to learn about what animals we might want and how to look after them but it didn't turn out that way.

'Guess what?' I burst in through the kitchen door and didn't give Michael time to answer. 'Garnet says he's willing to rent us two bits of land. The field down behind the barns and the other one on the opposite side of the lane.'

'I never expected that.'

'I know. He says we can have it right away. But only if we get some stock on it quickly as he doesn't want it going wild.'

'What stock? We haven't got any stock.'

I sat down at the kitchen table. 'What about those Jacob sheep at the farm on the back road? We could go and knock on their door and see if they'd sell us a couple of ewes. Just to get us started. Before he changes his mind.'

Two days later we found ourselves looking at a pen of Jacob

sheep, trying to decide which ones we should buy.

'Any of them leaping out at you?' I asked Michael quietly.

'Nope. They all look the same to me.'

We were woefully ignorant, with no idea as to what we should be looking for in a sheep. One of them lifted her head up and looked me straight in the eye, an unusual thing for a sheep as they often seemed somehow unfocused, as if they're not quite all there.

'We'll have that one please. And that one over there.'

And so the deal was done, a price agreed and the farmer offered to pop them in his trailer and deliver them the next day.

'That was very decisive,' said Michael as we drove back home. 'What made you choose those two?'

'One had nice eyes. The other one looked a bit thin and I felt sorry for it.'

'I'm not sure those are the soundest of reasons for selecting sheep.'

'If we'd dithered any longer we'd have looked like numpties who didn't know what they were doing.'

'God forbid anyone should think that.'

'Exactly. Now we've got twenty-four hours to find out how to look after a sheep.'

Of course it took a great deal longer than twenty-four hours. You could spend a lifetime learning about sheep and they would still come up with some mysterious ailment that flummoxed you or they would simply die on you despite all your best efforts. I spent long evenings poring over books, reading about how to choose a sheep, the day-to-day care, what to feed and when, how to manage the grazing, how to spot signs that a sheep was unwell and what to do about it.

'It says here that when you're buying a sheep there are various important things to look out for. Healthy feet, healthy teeth. The top and bottom jaws should be aligned. If the lower jaw is too short, which is known as "parrot mouth", or being "overshot", the sheep may have difficulty grazing a short pasture.' I looked at the picture in the book and had the uncomfortable feeling that it reminded me of one of our new sheep.

'We shall have to regularly trim their feet, worm them, clip their back ends, and shear them once a year. And the list of illnesses is simply huge.' I put my finger on the top of the paragraph and picked out a few that caught my eye. 'Blue tongue, pulpy kidney disease, bloody scours, dysentery, watery mouth, foot rot, grass staggers, pneumonia, arthritis, ringworm and rabies. Oh and here's one you'll like.' I looked over the top of my glasses at Michael. 'Pizzle rot. What do you think that means?'

'Do I really need to know?'

'Yes. It's an infection of the sheath area in a ram. A rotting penis.'

Michael screwed up his face in disgust.

'And then they can get ticks, lice, bot flies and maggots.'

'I shouldn't get too worried. You can't be expected to know all of those things and if there's a problem, we just call the vet.'

'From the looks of this list the vet would end up moving in. And cost us a fortune. Apparently you need to be able to sort most of it out yourself. The vet is the last resort. So I shall need to learn how to inject medication and how to stick a syringe down their throats without choking them to death.'

I sat back in my chair and rubbed my eyes. 'If I'd known all of that when we first started this I'd have run a mile in the opposite direction. And I haven't even started the chapters on choosing a ram, breeding, feeding and lambing.'

'You'll get the hang of it.' Michael was still sounding irritatingly unconcerned. He had his head buried in a book about pigs, which was a future project. 'Pigs seem much easier.'

Ideas that may seem simple on first impression rarely stay that way. The devil is always in the detail. There is some truth in the saying that 'ignorance is bliss' but when you take on the care and management of animals on a farm or smallholding, which usually means restricting their freedom and, as a consequence, altering the natural habits they would follow if left completely wild, you become responsible for their well-being. Ignorance was a luxury we could not afford. Ignorance can cost lives, a hard lesson we would learn over the coming years.

However, for the moment we had a period of respite, a few months to settle down, buy a few more ewes and get ourselves ready for the lambing cycle. And do a lot more reading.

Chapter 2

The turning of the seasons

I have always been acutely aware of the changing seasons. On one level they are simply a part of everyday life, unquestioned and taken for granted, like the sun and the moon, like day and night, and yet the individual character of each season influenced my moods on a day-to-day basis and coloured the way I felt about my life through each month of the year. Once we began to keep animals and attempted to grow our own vegetables, that connection to the natural world gained a new dimension.

The reason we have seasons at all is due to a collision between Earth and a planet the size of Mars some four and half billion years ago. That collision caused the Earth to tilt on its axis and is responsible for the climate-moderating seasons that we experience today.[1]

That is the scientific explanation but Greek mythology offers a more colourful version. When Hades stole Persephone to be his queen of the Underworld, her mother Demeter, the goddess of the harvest, was so distraught that she caused all the crops on Earth to die. A compromise was reached which allowed Persephone to spend spring and summer with her mother and the natural world flourished again in tune with her happiness at having her daughter returned to her. Due to a bit of underhand dealing by Hades, Persephone had to return to him for a certain portion of the year (exactly how long varies with different sources but it is broadly in line with autumn and winter) and, as Demeter mourned, so we humans had to endure a time of harsh weather where few plants would grow.

Traditionally, spring begins on March 20th, summer on June 21st, autumn starts on September 22nd and winter on December 21st. A leap year may move the dates one day forward. In the meteorological world of weather forecasting a recognised set date for recording data is required so their seasons are split up into four periods made up of three months each – for example March, April and May for spring – and each season begins on the first day of the month.

---

[1] Gemma Tarlach, '20 things you didn't know about seasons', March 2019, Discover Magazine, https://www.discovermagazine.com/environment/20-things-you-didnt-know-about-seasons

My own awareness of when each season began and ended never quite fitted into any of those parameters, but it was always the arrival of autumn that I was most keenly aware of. There was usually a day in late August when some inner, subconscious body clock told me that a subtle line had been crossed. The air felt sharper, and the light on the hills in the evening had a different intensity to it.

For many people trees are the most obvious manifestation of the different seasons, with the fresh greens of spring, the reds and golds of autumn, and the bare branches of winter, but it was the bracken that marked the changes most for me: irrepressible, invasive and largely seen as a pest by the farming community. As the broad swathes of bracken that covered our hills slowly died back each autumn, turning from green to fox-red, the mellow evening light transformed the dying plants into something else altogether, a sumptuous, copper-coloured cloak shot through with strands of bronze and gold, draped gracefully around the barren shoulders of the mountains. In the short winter days when the world around me seemed to have faded to shades of grey, black and white it was the bracken that would still retain a hint of colour, a reminder of what had been and what would come again. And on those cold, frosty mornings when we had to break the ice on the animals' water troughs and buckets, the bracken fronds turned into fantastical ice sculptures, delicate and incredibly beautiful. In late spring the whole cycle started again, green shoots resolutely pushing their way out of the barren earth, unfurling and carpeting the hills once more.

Now that our lives were governed by our smallholding calendar the turning of the seasons took on a greater significance, with new rituals and rhythms to follow and to understand. Autumn was tupping time, which is the word that describes the process of putting the ram in with the ewes so that they can mate. It was also the time when we filled our shelves with chutneys and jams, harvested our vegetables and filled the freezer with meat. In the winter we hunkered down and hibernated, digging up the last of the crops from our vegetable beds and leaving them tidy for the barren months to come as well as making sure we had enough feed and hay for the animals. In the spring life burst forth all around us and it was time for lambing, for planting, a season of hope and new beginnings. In summer our thoughts turned to making hay and shearing the sheep, to village shows and a brief time of respite.

And each year the cycle would begin again, timeless and enduring, each season bonding us ever more closely to the rhythms of the natural world in a way that was simply not possible in an urban existence.

The writer Eithne Massey sums this relationship up perfectly in her book *The Turning of the Year – Lore and Legends of the Irish Seasons*.

'Each of the seasons has a different energy, and different

task, pastimes, animals and plants associated with it. Each one has a different way of being, a different relationship with the earth. We mark these differences in every aspect of our lives, from the clothes we wear to the food we eat, in our celebrations and holidays and in the dark times when we trudge through each day, hoping that we are heading in the direction of the light.'[2]

We measure not just the passing of each year by the seasons, but also the different phases of our lives. None of us can escape the circle of life, the progression through the youth and innocence of our spring, to the summer of growing and learning, on to the wisdom of our autumnal years and finally to the winter when we fade away. We may all go through the same process but we make those seasons our own, a personal journey of discovery.

---

[2] Eithne Massey, *The Turning of the Year: Lore and Legends of the Irish Seasons*, The O'Brien Press, Kindle location 158.

Chapter 3

Chicken addiction

Some people collect antiques or paintings. During our smallholding years I became an avid collector of chickens, so much so that it almost grew into an addiction, and one that took me completely by surprise.

We began our relationship with chickens in the normal way, buying a couple of layers to provide us, and our B&B guests, with fresh eggs. Anyone who has kept free-range chickens will know that these eggs are very different to the commercially produced version. The yolks are a rich, golden yellow and they are bursting with flavour. This was reason enough to think chickens were wonderful, but then I went to my first chicken auction and realised that there was so much more to enjoy.

There is always a sense of energy and anticipation at auctions, regardless of whether they are selling properties or livestock. The sellers are keen to put on a good show and get the best price they can, whilst the buyers are hunting for bargains. Key to the success of the day is the auctioneer, the master of ceremonies, and he, or she, is expected to bring a sense of theatre to the proceedings. People are here to be entertained as well as to part with their money.

I loved the drama of it all, and told myself I was only going to have a day out, and to marvel at the number of different breeds of birds on show, creatures that were far removed from the humble, rather ordinary, laying hen. The Poultry Club of Great Britain lists 104 pure breeds on its website, but there are far more than that when you include the hybrids and cross-breeds. Many have names that are as strange, beautiful, ugly or charming as the birds themselves; the Frizzles and Silkies are fluffy creatures who look as if they've been put under a hairdryer on turbo-power, whilst the striking black and white Appenzeller Spitzhauben is the bird world's version of a Dalmatian. The Rumpless Araucana appears to have lost its back end and looks suitably weird without it, whilst the Poland could be a contender for Ladies Day at Ascot with its elegant furry white hat. The rather aggressive-looking Ko Shamo and Yamato Gunkei could have come straight out of an oriental cock-fighting pit and, at the other end of the scale, the gentle miniature Pekins, one of my favourites, waddle about with their fluffed-up legs. It was the sheer other-worldliness of all these birds that I found so fascinating.

I knew that we didn't need any more chickens, and that these fancy birds were often not good layers, and yet somehow, never quite knowing how it had happened, I would find myself catching the eye of the auctioneer and before I knew it I'd purchased a set of three Blue Pekin bantams for the bargain price of £45. Well, it felt like a bargain to me and if the seller felt that the auctioneer had done a good job and got top price, then we all went home happy.

I wasn't interested in showing or competing, I simply liked having chickens around. They were busy birds by nature, spending most of their time pecking and scratching for food, and yet they also loved to indulge themselves, stretching out their wings in the sunlight or wriggling around in chicken ecstasy in a dust bath. They proved to be intensely curious, and on the odd occasion when their gate was left open, I would soon find a chicken in my kitchen, cocking its head on one side, beady eyes on the lookout for something tasty.

As I spent time with them it became apparent that they had their own personalities and relationships with each other. There was an order as to who went into the henhouse first at night, with each bird having its place. Any individual thinking to change the way things were done was soon taught otherwise, but once the pecking order was established the flock was largely peaceful and well ordered.

We kept our birds in a field that adjoined our garden. This

field was owned by one of the long-established sheep-farming families in the village. At the bottom of this field, immediately behind our house, there was a separate L-shaped strip of land, part of which they used as a collection area to pen the sheep before taking them to market. We had asked our neighbour if we could buy or rent the short side of the L-shape as it butted up to our garden and they didn't use it, but they had said that they didn't want to part with it. However, they were happy for us to have the free use of it provided we fenced it off at our own expense.

Looking back I can see that this was a neighbourly act, a way of welcoming us to the village, but at the time we couldn't understand why they wouldn't sell us such a tiny, tiny piece of land that they were allowing to go wild. Renting, or being given the use of a space, is not the same as owning it. You, and your animals, are vulnerable if the landowner decides they no longer want you there. There was also a sense of being beholden, and we would rather have paid something than have it for nothing. It didn't feel quite right.

It took us a long time to understand the mindset of the farming community around us. For many of them the fields they owned had been in the family for generations, often hard-won through years of scrimping and saving, handed down from grandfather to father to son, or daughter, and they were not something to be given away lightly to a complete stranger. It wasn't really about the money, it was about inheritance, about local standing as well as a sense of history and their place in it. We had been in the village for less than a year and it would take a lot longer than that to build the relationships and trust that might persuade them to part with a tiny trinket from the treasure that they hoarded so fiercely. A friend who had a cottage further down the valley told us that it took twenty years before the local landowner was prepared to sell him a few extra metres to extend his garden. As the years passed and we got to know these families a little better I began to understand their way of thinking, and to accept that we would probably never own any land here. The answer was to be grateful that we had the use of our chicken patch under whatever terms were offered, rather than to waste time and energy fretting over the unattainable.

Michael built our first henhouse himself, a wooden box big enough for eight hens with a ramp for access. It had an electronic door, controlled by a timer, that was raised and lowered on a pulley at set times of the day. This door represented freedom and safety: freedom for us because it meant one of us didn't have to drive back and shut the chickens in for the night when we were halfway through a meal with friends several miles away, and safety for the hens as the local fox population caused havoc around all the smallholdings on a regular basis. There was no question of not shutting our girls in at night. They happily went to bed of their own volition and the door worked a treat, a gadget that was worth having.

It soon became obvious that our little henhouse was not big enough to accommodate our ever-growing number of hens. We bought a garden shed and fitted it out with nest boxes and perches. According to my many chicken books it was considered a bad idea to mix different types of chickens together, and they advised that introducing new birds to an established flock could cause aggressive behaviour, if not outright war, between the different factions. One of the well-known tricks of the trade was to quietly introduce new birds into the henhouse at night once the hens were asleep. By the morning the established flock would assume the newcomers had always been there and would accept them more readily. Given that chickens aren't completely stupid I found it hard to believe this subterfuge would work, but it certainly seemed to help and so my charming collection of layers and ornamental birds, full size and bantam, as well as some rescued commercial laying hens, all muddled along quite happily together.

Michael had become resigned to me returning from the auctions with a big cardboard box and a guilty look on my face, so when I came back empty-handed one afternoon he was surprised.

'I don't believe it. No chickens?'

'Not exactly,' I said, pulling an egg box out of my bag.

'Don't tell me you've been buying eggs. We've got more

than we know what to do with.'

'These eggs aren't for eating. They're fertilised. Bluey has gone broody again and I thought we could try and hatch our own. These are Barnevelder eggs so they will look different to Bluey but she'll still be happy to raise them.'

'And we want Barnevelders because…?'

'Because they are beautiful.' I ignored his sceptical look. 'And they're good layers. And very friendly.'

We put Bluey into a separate run where she wouldn't get bothered by the other birds and where we could make sure she had easy access to food and water, and then put the eggs under her. We watched and we waited and twenty-one days later we came down one morning to find that we had two new chicks to add to our family.

I defy anyone not to go a little gooey inside at the sight of a chick. We kept finding excuses to look at them, taking our morning coffee or an evening glass of wine, watching as these tiny beings copied everything that Bluey did. They were tricoloured balls of fluff, daubed with blobs of black and brown, but not yet recognisable as the adult bird they would grow to be. After two weeks they had doubled in size, after four weeks they were three times as big, and by six weeks they had a full body of feathers. By eight weeks they were classed as young adults with a lace-like brown and black feather pattern, wonderfully intricate, glossy and rich in tone with an iridescent sheen to it. Even

Michael had to admit that they were indeed very striking birds.

It's difficult to sex a chicken, but at some point we began to realise that we had our first cockerel in the family. Barnie grew into a giant of a bird, handsome and proud, but then he turned into a bully. Barnevelders are known for their docile good nature, even the cockerels, but Barnie must have missed out on those genes. He wasn't aggressive towards us, but he terrorised the other birds, particularly the bantams. He had a particular obsession with our little Pencilled Wyandotte, whom we had imaginatively named Pencil. She was so small she could stand underneath him and her head would hardly reach his belly. I think it would have been physically impossible for him to have his wicked way with her, but that didn't stop him trying, and getting vicious when it didn't go to plan.

We came home one day to find Pencil had escaped the chicken enclosure and was floating like a plastic duck on the small pond in the garden, looking very sorry for herself.

'What on earth is she doing there?' asked Michael. 'I thought hens hated water.'

A hen's feathers are not waterproof. Once they get sodden they will sink like a stone if anywhere near water deep enough to drown in. If they are not dried out quickly they get hypothermia and can die.

'I imagine she was trying to escape that bloody cockerel again,' I said as I got down on all fours and gently pulled Pencil towards me. 'She's shaking.'

We wrapped her in a towel and gently rubbed her but the water had soaked right through to her skin.

'How about I put the fan oven on its lowest setting? Maybe the warm air will circulate and dry her out.'

'That would be fine if we were going to eat her.' Michael looked at me incredulously.

'Don't be daft. She won't actually go in the oven. We'll sit her on the open door and see if the heat wafts out enough to warm her up. Let's give it a go.'

Pencil was normally a feisty little bird, not the easiest to handle, but she didn't move as I picked her up, put her on a baking tray and then slid it onto the open door.

We watched anxiously.

'Can you smell something?' asked Michael. 'A sort of singed smell?'

'Perhaps this wasn't a good idea,' I admitted.

'You don't say,' said Michael.

'It might be nice if you could come up with something useful instead of stating the obvious.'

I took Pencil away from the oven and sat her back down on her towel. Chickens don't have particularly expressive faces but I had the niggling feeling that there was just the hint of reproach in those glassy eyes. 'We've got to do something.' Then inspiration struck. 'A hairdryer, that will do the trick.'

This time, thankfully, my idea worked. Pencil was treated to a very thorough blow-dry. Michael held her in case she objected to such treatment and tried to peck at me, whilst I lifted her feathers and systematically dried her from the skin outwards.

'She looks better.' I sat back on my heels. 'We'll keep her here tonight. I'll leave her with a bit of grain and see how she is in the morning.'

The next morning Pencil was back to her old self, looking very cross at being confined in a small box and trying to peck at me as I lifted her out.

'You are a bad-tempered little hen, aren't you? I'm glad you're better though.'

I put her in a small run that we kept as a sick bay for the birds when needed and walked over to look at the rest of the flock. Michael joined me and watched Barnie as he pecked viciously at a passing Welsummer.

'That bird is a nightmare.' Michael sighed. 'What's wrong with him?'

'I don't know but he's pushed his luck too far this time. We had a happy, peaceful flock before he came along. He'll have to go.'

'Where to?'

'I'll put him in for the next auction. Perhaps he'll be better if he goes to a different flock, one without so many bantams.'

And so Barnie left us, and I had the unusual experience of coming away from an auction with one less bird than I had before I arrived.

Chapter 4

Oh, for a crystal ball

❖ ❖ ❖

There have been very few times in my life when I have wished for a crystal ball, few times when I would have been grateful to have been warned of a possible future so that I could decide whether to take the necessary steps to avoid it. It's often the most inconsequential decisions that send us down one route as opposed to another, and there are usually diversions that might allow us to escape this particular destiny if we only recognised them for what they were. But invariably we don't see any of this until after the event. Hindsight has ever been one of the most irritating words in the dictionary as it always comes too late to be of any use.

It all began with an opportunity. As we settled into the village we made new friends and two of these friends offered us the use of their field. The rent was minimal as what they really wanted was for the land to be grazed and kept under control.

'This would give us enough land for Snari,' said Michael. 'Maybe we can take him out of livery. All he needs is a field shelter. It would be great to have him so close to us.'

Snari was Icelandic for 'speedy'. Perhaps he had shown a turn of speed as a foal but now, most of the time, he was a steady and calm horse. This is the only breed of horse allowed in Iceland. All others are banned in a bid to keep the breed pure and, now that Snari had left, he would never be allowed back. I sometimes wondered if he missed his homeland, but that was one of those questions that we shall never know the answer to.

The Icelandic horse is part of the national identity and with one horse for every four people in Iceland, 80,000 in total, they are a common sight. Another 100,000 have been exported around the world, although if you are not interested in horses you may never have heard of them.

'He'll need some company,' I said. 'I can get a horse too.'

It seemed the perfect idea. I'd never had my own horse, but I'd spent most of my childhood at the local stables and had been dipping in and out of riding ever since. Michael began work on the field shelter and I started to look for my dream horse.

I soon learnt that there are reasons why people are selling their allegedly much-loved animal and they don't always share those reasons with you. The first horse I tried saw demons in every hedgerow and went sideways more often than forward, the second had a debilitating skin condition that cost a fortune to medicate and meant it couldn't be ridden for long periods of time, and the third had a malicious tendency to throw in a buck just as its rider was getting on, expertly timed for when you were at your most vulnerable with only one foot in the stirrup. Things finally seemed to be improving with the fourth horse, a handsome chestnut Welsh cob called Red, but by now I was becoming very sceptical about the whole process. The owner understood my reticence and was happy for me to get to know the horse at her home before I committed to anything. I rode out with her as company to start with and then by myself. I groomed him, mucked him out and collected him from the field, always on the lookout for bad habits. After three weeks I felt more confident and so I bought him.

We introduced him to Snari and they got along extremely well. We left them together for a few days so that Red could settle in properly and then we saddled up for our first ride together. Our field was half way up the side of a steep hill, the only way down being along a rough, single-track road with open land to either side. Red and I began to make our way gently down to the bridle tracks below, with Michael following behind on Snari.

I could feel straight away that something was different.

Red's gait was short and choppy and he shook his head restlessly, pulling hard on the bit. Seconds later he broke into a trot and I felt his back twist beneath me. If we had been on the flat, or even at the bottom of the hill, I might have been able to bring him back or just push him through it up the slope. With hindsight I should have walked him down on a lead rein and saddled up at the bottom, but hindsight wasn't around on that day. As he picked up speed, fighting me, he slipped on the road and I could feel his back legs sliding beneath him.

That was all it took. He began to buck, little ones to start with but then they got bigger. To this day I shall never know if he wanted me off his back or if he panicked in new surroundings. I felt myself lift out of the saddle, too far to come back down again, and knew I had passed the point of no return. There was a sense of weightlessness, a panicky wonder at being airborne, quickly replaced by a sense of shock at how quickly this had happened, and the next thing I knew I was lying flat on my back on the grass, winded and gasping for breath.

Seconds later Michael appeared, hovering over me, anxiety written all over his face.

'Are you all right?'

'I'm not sure.'

'Does anything hurt? Can you move? Should I call an ambulance?'

'I think I just need to lie here for a bit. Where's Red?'

'Close by. Once you were off he seemed to calm down. You look very pale.'

I wiggled my toes and fingers, turned my neck, lifted my

arms. Nothing seemed out of place so with Michael's help I tentatively pushed myself up into a seating position. From there I could see Red halfway down the hill.

'That bloody horse is grazing. Like nothing happened.'

Michael put his arm around me and helped me stand. As soon as I put my weight on my right leg I felt a shooting pain through my ankle.

'Ouch! I think I've sprained it.'

We decided that I would sit and rest a while longer whilst Michael put both horses back in the field. By the time he came back I felt a bit better and was able to hobble back down to the house. My ankle was uncomfortable and I knew I was going to have bruises all down my back by the following day but my overwhelming emotion was one of relief. It could have been so much worse.

After an uncomfortable night I woke to find my ankle swollen. I had initially thought to take it easy for a few days and leave it at that, but a nursing friend suggested that I should get it x-rayed, just to be on the safe side. The x-ray showed that I had fractured a bone in my ankle, the talus, and would need to be in plaster, non-weight bearing, and on crutches for a minimum of three months. This bone was not a particularly good one to break as it allowed the foot to move inwards and outwards, important for walking on uneven ground. If the bone didn't knit back together by itself over those three months then it would need surgery to realign it and a metal plate and pins to hold it in place. The surgeon was also concerned that there might be a problem with blood supply to the fracture, which could cause the bone to die, leading to deformity and a painful condition to live with. All we could do for the moment was to wait and see what happened over the next three months, after which there would be more scans to evaluate what progress had been made.

Both Michael and I had genuinely convinced ourselves that it was a simple sprain and that I would be back on my feet again in a week or so. I can still vividly picture the shock on Michael's face and assume I must have looked the same.

Everything we did in our lives, the business, the B&B, the animals, we did together. Now we had to adapt to the reality that a great deal of that was going to fall on Michael's shoulders. I soon learnt that I hadn't just lost the use of a leg for those months, but I had also lost the use of my hands because of the crutches. The most ordinary and simple things became incredibly difficult. When you have no free hands and only one useable leg, something as simple as making a cup of tea and carrying it to the sofa becomes a major logistical exercise. The arthritis in my hands didn't appreciate having to take all my weight and so I couldn't walk far on my crutches which left me screaming inside with frustration and a sense of loss. I never truly valued the freedom of walking in my beloved hills until I couldn't do it any more. And at night, unable to sleep well with the plaster on my leg, I would lie awake and wonder what would happen if the bone didn't mend.

In the end I was in plaster for three and half months and the bone mended without needing to be pinned. It was months after that before I could walk without pain but eventually I was pretty much back to normal. However I found that I was more cautious when walking out in the mountains, much slower over rocky terrain and down steep slopes, and that caution has never left me. Red went back to his owners, although they would have been quite within their rights not to accept him, but they were horrified at what had happened and, able to see that it would be months before I could ever ride again, if indeed I would be able to ride at all, they preferred to take him back. I was grateful for their understanding as I eventually came to the conclusion that my riding days were over – I didn't bounce like I used to.

I have nothing good to say about those frustrating, worrying months in plaster and the time spent recovering my mobility. They say every cloud has a silver lining but I couldn't find one in this particular cloud, no matter how hard I looked. However it did teach me a couple of things.

It taught me that small kindnesses can give a disproportionately large amount of comfort and strength, far more than the giver of those kind thoughts and acts could ever know. Friends and family rang me far more regularly than usual, just to check that my spirits were up. One friend would bundle me and my crutches into the car and take me out for a trip when I seemed overly glum, whilst another friend marched into the kitchen one day with a list of herbal remedies, determined to speed the mending process up. One of these herbal solutions was comfrey, also known as 'knitbone' and I am convinced that it made a real difference to the healing process.

The most important thing I learnt was that I could rely on Michael to be there for me, unreservedly, totally, utterly. He took on the burden of juggling all the different aspects of our lives and never once moaned about it. And when I had a bad-tempered moment, or a day, or ended up in floods of tears of angry frustration because I'd spilt my mug of tea in an unbalanced moment on my crutches, his answer was to simply give me a hug until the tears or the tantrum stopped. A good hug goes a long way.

Perhaps learning these things was my silver lining.

Chapter 5

Ram

❖ ❖ ❖

In the world of sheep breeding there is a line of thought that says that the ram is the heart of the flock. It is his genes that will produce strong, sound progeny and establish a successful bloodline. I could see the sense of this, but it seemed to me to be only half the story because surely the ewe also needed to be of good stock. With that in mind we had bought two more Jacob ewes from an established breeder. They were pedigree sheep registered with the Jacob Sheep Society and came complete with a certificate that traced their bloodlines. Breeding is a serious business and pedigree sheep are given long and fancy names that we couldn't begin to cope with. Instead we called one Morag as she had Scottish connections in her ancestry and the other one by the cruelly undignified name of Fatso, simply because she was huge, even before she swelled up with lambs.

Our two pedigree girls had to slum it with our first purchase of two local sheep who were anything but pedigree. One of these I called Lady Eleanor, shortened to Ellie, and she was always one of my favourites as she had a steady, gentle dignity about her, and the other was just Missie.

With our starter flock in place and autumn approaching it was time to think about putting our girls to the ram. The larger sheep farmers will keep their own rams, who lie around doing very little for most of the year and then run themselves ragged with the irrepressible urge to jump on any passing ewe who is giving off the right hormones. Pedigree rams can cost a great deal of money. The world's most expensive ram was sold for an eye-watering £367,500 in 2010 in Scotland. He went by the suitably grand name of Sportsmans Double Diamond and was bought by a group of three farmers. He was just six months old, a huge, pug-nosed Texel, and it's just as well sheep have no concept of value because if he knew how much they'd paid for him, and what high expectations came with it, I doubt he'd have been able to perform his duties at all.

At the other end of the scale we could have bought a Jacob ram of considerably less distinguished breeding for £100. We decided against doing this as we didn't have the spare land for him to live on for the rest of the year. This is often the case for the smaller farmers or smallholders and so rams are borrowed for the month or so that they are needed. I liked to think of it as the 'rent-a-ram' scheme.

As we were now members of the Jacob Sheep Society we contacted them and asked if they could put us in touch with a flock owner in the area who would be willing to lend us a ram. They gave us the telephone number of a farmer who said she had a couple of young rams which might suit us. We were welcome to come and have a look and choose one.

We borrowed a sheep trailer from friends in the hopeful expectation that we would be returning with a ram and, as we rattled our way along the back lanes, I ran through a mental checklist of what we should be looking for.

Most of it was exactly the same as looking for a ewe. The animal should have good teeth, healthy feet with no cracking, and be sound and alert. The Jacob breed typically would have a deep body, straight back, and a white blaze down the middle of the face. If I wanted to be picky there were lots of other small points about its black and white markings but I wasn't too concerned about that. I was breeding them for meat, not to win shows. The horns, whether two or four, should grow upwards from the head, not forwards. Lastly, and perhaps most importantly, there were the testicles.

I had seen prospective buyers at auctions gently squeezing a ram's testicles and, from hours of reading up on the subject, knew that they were checking to see if they were firm, evenly sized and moved around freely within the scrotum. I didn't feel qualified to judge whether a ram's testicles were good, bad or indifferent. I guess there is a first time for everything but I hadn't made my mind up yet whether I would be doing this.

We arrived at what we hoped was the address, a gated lane in the middle of nowhere, pulled the Land Rover and trailer off the road, and walked in. First impressions weren't promising.

A track led up to an unkempt bungalow facing an assortment of barns and sheds that were leaning up against each other in a bid not to fall down. The yard was littered with what looked like the leftovers from a greengrocer stall, bits of lettuce and carrot, various greens and root vegetables, and there were chickens everywhere, squabbling as they fought over the choicer titbits. Dotted about in the long grass in front of the bungalow, where once there had been a lawn, I counted at least ten chicken runs with a mother hen and chicks in each one, all of different breeds and different ages.

I rang the doorbell but there was no answer, then knocked loudly on the door. Still no answer.

'What should we do?' I double-checked the time on my watch. 'She should be expecting us.'

'There are more sheds out the back. Maybe she's in there.'

Things became ever more dilapidated the further we went. The owner obviously didn't have either the money or the inclination to repair and maintain the property. I began to wonder what state of health the sheep would be in. The door to one of the bigger sheds was half open. Michael pushed it open further and we called out.

'Anybody there?'

It was dark inside the barn, the only light coming from weak strands of daylight creeping in through broken slats in the wooden walls. As our eyes adjusted we saw that the barn had been divided into pens, each of them housing four or five turkeys.

'Come on in,' a voice called. 'I'm at the back.'

We could just make out a figure at the rear of the barn, bent over a single turkey separated from the others in a small pen. As we approached she looked up.

'Pass me that tub, will you?' She gestured at a pot of medication perched on a wooden beam. I handed it to her and we both watched as she smeared it gently over a seeping infection on the bird's leg.

'This bird is on its last legs. Literally.' She dropped the tin back on the shelf in disgust, wiping her hands on the front of her overalls. 'I've tried everything but I think it's got the better of me.'

We followed her back out into the yard and took stock of each other. She was a small, wiry woman, probably in her early sixties, with iron-grey hair bundled carelessly into a ponytail. She gave us one of those assessing looks that people who know a lot about animals give to those who obviously don't. I stifled an internal sigh and wondered whether there would ever come a day when a newbie sheep owner would come to me for advice, rather than it always being the other way round.

'You'll be wanting a ram then. This your first time?'

We nodded.

'They're in the field. Follow me.'

The sheep were in a small field of a similar size to the one we rented, but where we had just four sheep in ours, there were easily thirty sheep in this one. There are well-documented rules about how many sheep should be grazed per acre to keep the grass fresh and the sheep healthy. This broke all those rules. The grass had been nibbled away to nothing.

'Wow, that's a lot of sheep,' I said, realising too late that it might be taken as a criticism.

'Too many sheep. Too many birds. Should get rid of the lot of them.' She didn't look at me as she said this, gazing instead into the field. 'I used to send a load off to the abattoir each year. Lost the appetite for it somewhere along the line.'

She opened the gate and we walked in amongst the flock. She pointed out various rams, discussing their age, their background and how easy they were to handle. The flock looked a lot better than I would have expected given the poor grazing and it soon became obvious that she knew a great deal about sheep. She had seemed taciturn on first impressions but the more time we spent with her, the more expansive she became, happy to answer all our questions.

'You won't go wrong with this one.' She pointed out a young ram. 'This is his first year so he's new to it all, a bit like you. It's taken him a while to get the hang of it, but he's keen.'

I ran my eye over him. He looked bright, with healthy feet and a thick fleece. His markings were good and, although he was on the small side, he was stocky and strong. His testicles hung below his belly. I walked around him and studied them from all angles. They looked fine to me.

'We'll take him.'

'Thirty quid all right with you? And you can have him for as long as you need.'

I nodded.

'Right. Let's get them penned and you can take him today.'

I had seen shepherds at the big livestock shows moving their sheep around effortlessly with just a whistle and a highly trained dog. From our experience of watching the farmers in Wales we soon realised that not everyone had that level of control. More often than not it was a noisy affair, with a gang of sheepdogs and a great deal of yelling, which invariably turned to swearing as the dogs decided to go their own way, scattering sheep in all directions.

I watched this diminutive woman as she single-handedly brought her flock in and realised I was getting a lesson in a different way of doing things. She was quiet, calm and unhurried, calling them in with her own particular sound, one I knew I might try and practise back at home and fail miserably at, and from the way they followed her I could see that this was a habit, built up over time and based on trust.

She singled out our ram and deftly manoeuvred him into a holding pen before he had time to realise what was happening. Standing in the trailer all by himself he looked even smaller, and seemed a bit lost. I wondered how animals felt when we took them away from their own kind and from their familiar habitat. This was a subject not really considered in any of my books on livestock, an omission that spoke volumes.

'You take good care of him and let me know if you have any problems. Give me a call when you're ready to bring him back.' And with that she turned and headed back to the barns, presumably to glare at the sick turkey until it either got better or died.

'That went better than I thought it might,' I said to Michael as we drove home, taking the corners slowly so as not to throw our new arrival around in the trailer. 'I wasn't sure it was going to work out when we arrived.'

'Me neither. Just goes to show that first impressions can be wrong.'

I nodded in agreement and wondered what age I would have to reach before I had the wisdom not to judge people too quickly. Money could buy expensive sheep sheds and plenty of land but it didn't guarantee a caring connection to the animals. If I had to guess I would say that the lady we had just met knew full well that she should downsize but couldn't bring herself to do it. It wasn't my business to judge.

'Just one question,' said Michael. 'Did I miss the bit where you palpated the testicles?'

'I decided to trust her judgement.'

'Shame. That would have been worth seeing.'

'Do you know you have the sense of humour of a twelve-year-old?'

'Oh yes,' he said proudly.

We arrived back home, unloaded the ram into the field and waited to see how everybody got along. The girls were absolutely delighted to see him. Their heads went up as we walked him into the field and within seconds they had surrounded him, sniffing and nosing at him.

'Poor bugger looks terrified,' said Michael.

And it was true he looked overwhelmed. They were all bigger than him and evidently quite excited by his presence.

'Hopefully he'll get used to them and start doing what he's here for,' I said, frowning as he ran off in the opposite direction with the girls chasing after him.

Rams are often called 'tups'. It's an ancient word, originating in the north of England in the Middle Ages. The productivity of a tup will depend on his age, experience, and the size of the field he is housed in. An experienced ram can typically cover five ewes in a day but this figure can vary depending on whether the ewes are experienced or first-timers, with the latter often requiring more effort on his part. The ewe will make the first move, seeking the ram out, but he has a narrow window of time to successfully impregnate her. Each cycle lasts seventeen days but there is a period of only twenty-four to thirty-six hours when she will stand for him. In the larger flocks, where the tups are having to work hard, a ewe might easily be missed and so it is common practice to keep a tup with the flock for two cycles, around thirty-four days.

Rams can lose up to 15% of their body weight during a tupping season, but our young lamb would have an easy time of it with such a small flock, once he got over first-date nerves. The only other slight concern was that some rams have a poor libido due to a lack of testosterone, whilst around 10% are homosexual and will not mate at all. The gestation period is on average 146 days, just over four and a half months, which would mean our lambing season would run from mid-March to mid-April next year. Time would tell how successful he had been. Until then, we would just let them get on with it.

Chapter 6

Loss

❖ ❖ ❖

Jessie was curled up in her basket, eyes closed, her grey muzzle resting on her paws. She was fourteen years old now and she wouldn't make fifteen. I knew we were coming to the end. Each night I stroked her head as I turned the lights out and went to bed, wondering if that was the last time I would be able to do that, wondering if she would have quietly drifted away as we slept upstairs and I would come down in the morning to find I had lost a dear companion.

A peaceful death was what I would have wished for her, for any of us, but I knew it was unlikely. Instead she would get sicker and frailer and at some point it would be up to me to make a decision that would break my heart.

I remembered when I first saw her, only a few weeks old, the unwanted result of an expensive pedigree black Labrador escaping for a quick fling with a local collie on the prowl. She was one of a litter of six, and I knew she was the one I wanted from the moment I set eyes on her. I took her home when she was eight weeks old, and we shared a few challenging months where she chewed anything she could get her teeth into: the usual things like socks and boots if I didn't remember to put them out of reach but also less obvious things like the wallpaper off the walls. My father and I built her an outside run but she dug her way out of that within days. There were times when I thought I'd brought a monster home, but those times soon passed. She calmed down and we became inseparable.

I was living alone at the time; my first marriage had just failed and I had moved to a different part of the country and begun a new career in landscape gardening. It would take me time to establish both the business and new friends, to build a whole new life for myself, and it was lonely to start with.

The bond between one dog and one person is a strong one. As soon as you introduce a second dog or another person, the relationship changes. In those early years it was just Jessie and me. She was my constant companion, jumping into the passenger seat of my little Bedford van each day, eager to get to work and meet some new people. In the evenings she sat at my feet by the fire, helping to turn a house into a home.

She was around twelve years old when I met Michael and she adored him. At around that time I decided to get a puppy and luckily found a collie cross in the village. Jessie knew how to behave with sheep, both our own and those we might meet out walking, and I thought it would help to train up a new dog with Jessie as her role model. Also, niggling away at the back of my mind, I knew that Jessie was coming towards the end of the road and couldn't bear the thought of being without a dog.

It was a slow decline, one little thing after another, each one taking its toll, each one pushing us closer to an inevitable conclusion. The normal signs of ageing, such as her arthritis, failing eyesight and deafness, we could manage. Then she started to get nosebleeds and dizzy spells. And finally she began to suffer from intermittent attacks that would make her walk round and round in tiny circles, seemingly unable to stop, becoming ever more distressed until something switched off in her brain and she would go back to normal. It was an awful thing to watch.

The vets ran a seemingly never-ending range of tests and we managed her conditions as best as we could but they warned us that it was only a matter of time. Her quality of life was diminishing fast.

That is the point we had reached as I stroked her head that night. In the following ten days the attacks started to come more regularly and lasted longer. Hardly a day went by without me contacting the vet, but there was nothing they could do. After yet another sleepless night I came downstairs one morning and phoned the vet to come out and put her down.

'Have I done the right thing?' I asked Michael miserably.

'You've done the right thing for *her*. It isn't fair to let her go on like this.' He looked at Jessie and sighed. 'It's never going to feel the right thing for us though.'

I knelt by her bed and stroked her soft ears. She seemed fine this morning, much calmer in herself.

'No. I can't do this. She seems better. I'll call the vet and tell him not yet.'

Michael put his hands on my shoulders and looked me straight in the eye. 'You've been saying that for days. You have to be strong.'

I nodded and stepped away from the phone. I had two hours to get through before the vet arrived and I suddenly needed to get out of the house. If I stayed there I knew I wouldn't be able to stop myself from calling the whole thing off.

'I'm going out for a walk, just to clear my head. Can you keep an eye on her for a bit?'

Michael nodded, his eyes full of concern.

I didn't go far, just down to the sheep field. I sat on my straw bale seat, watched the sheep rhythmically and mindlessly chewing away and tried to let that calm emptiness wash over me. It didn't work today. I got up and began to pace up and down, hardly aware that I was doing it, telling myself over and over again all the reasons why this was the right thing to do. As a dog owner, the final act of love for your dog, and a responsibility you must eventually face up to, is to make sure it doesn't suffer. I repeated this to myself like some kind of cursed mantra and then I sat back down and cried my eyes out until I felt drained and empty. Finally I went back to the house and sat with my dog until the vet arrived.

He was a young vet, but knowledgeable, good at his job, and he had got to know both us and Jessie well over the last few months. Michael and I sat close together on the sofa, stroking Jessie, while he administered the drug, and she slowly and peacefully left us. But before he began, he looked at me and said something for which I shall be eternally grateful.

'You're doing the right thing.'

Six little words, but his endorsement of this horrible act gave me great relief and lessened the burden of guilt and anxiety.

We buried her in the garden and life went on as it always does. But it was a long time before I stopped expecting to see her waiting for me when I came home and whilst I've had two other much-loved dogs since then, neither of them stole my heart the way she did.

Chapter 7

One door closes, another opens

❖ ❖ ❖

The dark days of winter pass so slowly. Each year I long for the spring. If the winter has been particularly harsh that longing teeters on the verge of desperation, and it seems that the older I get the harder it is to find very much that is positive about those cold wet months. There were times when the weather in our Welsh mountains could be extreme enough to take on its own personality, a hostile, angry being that pounded both the land and the humans that lived on it. I sympathised with the goddess Demeter. As she mourned her daughter at this time of year, I mourned a benign world where the air was soft on my face, where I could look out of my window and marvel at how many shades of green nature creates on her palette as she paints her vibrant pictures of springtime.

As February turned into March I prowled around the garden,

scanning the borders for the first sign of daffodils poking their heads out of the cold earth. In the wild hedgerow along the lane there was a particular hawthorn bush which came out before all others and each morning as I walked past I looked at it anxiously, hoping to see those first green shoots, reassurance that nature was coming out of hibernation and that all was as it should be.

The word 'spring' comes from the verb 'to spring' and is associated with things springing into life. Officially spring begins on March 20th, but the weather patterns in our Welsh hills were notoriously fickle at this time of year and so the beginning of spring in real life tended to be a moveable feast.

The springtime meant one thing above all others in the smallholding calendar – lambing. In previous years my awareness of springtime had been centred around plants, flowers and trees. This would be our first year of lambing so that awareness was going to expand into new lives of a four-legged nature. I was both excited and terrified in equal measure.

Because we had been in such a hurry last year to get some sheep into our newly rented field we had chosen Jacob sheep without even considering the many other breeds available. It turned out that we had made a good choice, albeit more by luck than judgement.

They are an ancient breed, first imported to the UK from Spain in the seventeenth and eighteenth century by the landed gentry, who used them as ornamental sheep to graze with the deer in the parklands surrounding their castles and stately homes. The oldest known flock from that time is still grazed at Charlecote Park in Warwickshire. There is no doubt that they are indeed striking in appearance, with their black and white fleeces and distinctive horns, either a pair of two horns which curl round and back on themselves or four, with the extra set straight and pointing up at the sky, always reminding me of the horn on a unicorn. As novice smallholders we deliberately chose the two-horn variety for our flock to avoid impaling ourselves on the sharp ends of the unicorn horns, but I always felt a niggling regret at that choice as there is nothing quite so magnificent as a mature four-horned Jacob ram.

While the names of many breeds of sheep are descriptive of their physical characteristics or an area of the country, Jacob sheep are named from a story told in the Old Testament book of Genesis. The story is a long and convoluted one, centred around a man called Jacob, his misadventures with his family and how he became a breeder of the spotted and pied sheep that are so instantly recognisable today.

By the beginning of the First World War many of the established flocks had disappeared, so much so that in 1969 the Jacob Sheep Society was formed to protect the breed. The organisation began with 96 members, but has grown from strength to strength and now has 850 members. It began with a total of 2,700 registered sheep, but these days a further 2,000 sheep are registered every year.

They are a hardy, self-sufficient breed, easily wintered outside, and have a greater natural resistance to disease and foot problems than some other breeds. Their meat is flavoursome and lean, whilst their wool is prized for spinning and weaving. Most importantly for us, they have a reputation for being excellent mothers, needing little help in the lambing process, and perfectly able to look after a set of triplets. They are also long-lived and it is not uncommon for them to still be raising lambs at seven years of age. Put all these features together and you have the perfect breed of sheep for a smallholder.

Our little rent-a-ram had obviously conquered his initial nerves as all our girls were now expecting lambs. Commercial sheep farmers, who may be expecting a thousand lambs or more, apply a combination of modern science and ancient folklore to pinpoint exact dates of conception, and from that point they can also predict birthing dates, so that they can organise their lambing season. Sheep will be scanned to determine whether they are carrying a single, twins or triplets so that their feeding regime can be controlled. In most cases the ewes are brought into barns so that it is easier to spot any problems and sort them out quickly and then they will be moved out to the lambing fields, leaving space for the next batch of ewes. They're not quite on a conveyor belt but it works on the same principles.

We had just four ewes, no recourse to science or scans, and

were going to play it by ear. Michael would hold the fort on work which meant that I was free to keep an eye on them, and we were under no pressure on timing. They would arrive when they arrived. With hindsight, we would soon be understanding exactly why you needed to have a reasonable idea of when the lamb was due if you wanted to get the correct feeding regime and have any sort of life of your own at all, but this was our first year and our only real goal was to get to the end of it without losing anyone. The fine-tuning could come later.

The last four to six weeks of pregnancy is when the majority of growth takes place and the feeding regime will determine the size and health of the lamb as well as the milk producing ability of the ewe. It is important to get it right and the art is in making sure not to feed too much, which will result in big lambs who are difficult to birth, or to feed too little which will result in frail lambs and could affect the ewe's milk supply. A ewe carrying a single will need less supplementary feeding than one carrying triplets. We looked at Fatso in particular with a sense of ever-increasing horror as she grew rounder and rounder.

'She's almost as wide as she is tall now,' said Michael. 'How many can she have in there?'

'God knows.' I shook my head. As the lambing date loomed nearer I was beginning to feel more and more out of my depth. There were so many things that could go wrong and I would have to make a quick decision as to whether it was something I could handle or whether the vet was needed. If a lamb presented badly with a leg tangled up, came out backwards in a breech birth or simply got stuck because it was too big, there would be no option but for me to go boldly forth where I had never been before. Once lubed up I would need to put my hand inside, work out which bit went where, rearrange it if possible and then gently ease the lamb out, trying to work with the contractions so as not to damage or hurt the ewe. An experienced sheep farmer would recognise the point where he needed to get the vet to intervene, but I didn't have any experience to guide me, just weeks of poring over books and diagrams. I tried to make myself feel better with the usual panaceas: everybody had to start somewhere, and the only way to get experience was to just do it, but they didn't take away the hard knot of worry that now accompanied my every visit to my flock, particularly in the early hours of the morning.

Some close friends of ours, Trish and Tony, had been sheep farming in this valley for thirty-eight years and Trish had some fascinating tales to tell of their early days. Like us, they had started with no previous experience, but seeing how much knowledge and experience they had amassed over those years gave me hope that eventually I too might reach a point where I would be equally competent. I spent many a happy time up at their farm, sharing the sofa with one or more of their dogs, listening spellbound as Trish told me stories about their early days.

'We *bought the farm with 100 ewes already on site. Lambing was learned on the hoof with a book called "The TV Vet Guide to Sheep Rearing" which was invaluable. Our neighbour, Ifor, taught us so much and we could rely on his advice if the book was not clear on something. Over the years we have learned to pull all kinds of lambs coming awkwardly: they should come out in diving position, nose first, then one little foot each side of the chin. If one leg is back, the shoulder can get stuck, so the ewe will need help. Usually you leave a ewe for a couple of hours to try for herself as intervention can cause more problems, but both legs back is a horrible problem and the quicker you get involved the better as, if left too long, the cervix will start to close and the head will swell before the lamb can be born.*

'*The first time we had one of these we were really puzzled as there was nothing seemingly to pull. It was early morning so we called a neighbour who said to load her up and bring her over. The poor man, who was in his mid-eighties, had been out all night with his own flock and was just off to bed as his son had taken over. We arrived with the ewe in the back of the Land Rover, he came out in his pyjamas, talked us through pulling the lamb, we returned with a very relieved ewe and he went back to bed!*

'*Tangled twins can be difficult as you have to work out which foot belongs to which head and which way is it coming, and back leg presentations have to be pulled quickly as the lamb* can drown in the birth liquid ... in fact no end of things can go wrong. Lambs that have died inside are horrid too; often the ewe simply can't throw them and just wanders about looking miserable. When you do manage to pull them out they can come out in bits, smelling ferociously foul. However four days of ampicillin, a drug which has similar properties to penicillin, usually sees the ewe back on her feet.'

It was from these conversations with Trish that I learnt how important it was to be aware of the different medications available to a sheep farmer and to be able to medicate your own flock. The cost of calling a vet out would be expensive enough for us as smallholders, but for farmers with large flocks it was prohibitive.

'Calcium and magnesium injections are amazing at curing twin lamb disease, which is caused mostly by a smaller ewe carrying twins and not eating enough. From being down and unable to feed her lambs, a 20cc injection is given inside each leg, and miraculously she is up in fifteen minutes.

'Ampicillin injections are essential following any intervention, and all the hill farmers have it on hand as calling a vet out is not financially viable. When we started a ewe was worth around £30 and a lamb £15. A vet would charge £25 just to come out, with any medications extra on top of that. Farmers all learn to fix their animals and their machines without professional help, aiding each other by sharing their knowledge. It is a good life.'

A few weeks previously I had enrolled myself onto a day course on lambing run by the local vets. They had rigged up a contraption to simulate a ewe in birth, basically a big bag with the right-sized opening in it, and had placed a newly deceased lamb inside so that we could all practise rearranging it and pulling it out. It felt distinctly macabre, and didn't do a great deal to improve my confidence.

There are well-documented signs that give a shepherd warning that a ewe is on the verge of giving birth. Her udder becomes engorged, her vulva red and swollen. She may separate herself from the flock and make herself a nest, restlessly pawing at the ground. The birth is imminent when she lies down, pushes her nose up in the air and begins to visibly strain and push.

As lambing draws ever closer the ewes need to be kept an eye on round the clock. I had been checking them last thing before I went to bed and getting up earlier in the morning, but now they needed a night-time visit. The alarm would jangle wildly at two am, my hand flapping and flailing to turn the accursed contraption off. Still half asleep, I would pull on some clothes and trudge down the lane to the sheep fields. Not once in that first lambing season was there anything to see, anything for me to deal with. As I shone my torch around the field, checking each sheep-shaped shadow, they paid me no attention whatsoever, just carried on munching or staring peacefully into space in the way that only sheep can do. I would stomp grumpily back up the lane with mixed feelings, partly relieved that everyone was fine, partly disappointed that I hadn't seen the miracle of a new life being born and partly irritated that I would have to drag myself out of bed again at the same time tomorrow morning, probably for nothing.

Ellie was the first to lamb and she presented me with a *fait accompli* when I arrived for my morning visit. She must have given birth sometime quite soon after my two am visit, although she had been showing no signs of doing so, because the lamb had been licked clean, was reasonably firm on its feet and already very clear on where it needed to go to find milk. My first view of it was its rump and its little tail, wiggling away with a mind of its own, as it sucked with total concentration on the teat. Ellie looked at me serenely, and I could almost imagine her telling me that there never had been anything to worry about. She knew exactly what she was doing.

Trish and Tony popped in to see our firstborn. I had penned Ellie and the lamb so that I could do the post-lambing checks. I had cut the umbilical cord and dipped it in iodine so that there was no chance of infection, checked that milk was flowing smoothly from both teats and given Ellie a bucket full of water, which she consumed as if she'd spent a week in the desert. I'd found the afterbirth and disposed of it so it couldn't attract a fox. Now she was munching contentedly on some hay whilst we stood around her and discussed what had happened. I knew I had a big grin on my face; it seemed to have become a permanent fixture, but they were smiling too.

'You must have seen this a thousand times,' I said. 'Does it ever become a bit run-of-the-mill? A bit ordinary?'

'Never,' said Trish. 'You can't beat the sight of a newborn lamb, especially if it's your own.'

'He's certainly got some timbers on him,' said Tony.

'What do you mean?' I asked.

He explained that when they bought their farm they didn't know much about sheep farming. Wandering around a ram sale in Builth Wells, they decided to listen carefully to what the old farmers were saying as they stood in small groups muttering knowledgeably about the penned sheep. One of the statements went along the lines of 'Just look at the timbering on that one. He'll do well for someone'. They asked the farmer what he meant by it and he said it showed that the ram had big, straight back legs and strong hips.

And that is how our first lamb came to be called Timber. He grew into a huge ram with a lovely nature and stayed with us right until the end.

A few days later Morag gave birth and this time I saw the whole thing. She'd taken herself off to the edge of the field, under the hedge, and was down on the ground, her nose in the air. I ducked back behind the barn. She was of a completely different nature to Ellie, so flighty and nervous that if she saw me, she'd probably run off and the last thing I wanted to do was to disturb her. Keeping my body out of sight, I craned my head around the corner, just enough to be able to see what was happening.

The first lamb slithered out a few minutes later, and lay on the ground. Morag turned around and began licking it enthusiastically, clearing the birth sac away from its mouth and nostrils first. With a bit of twitching and jerking the lamb found its feet and then promptly fell over. Morag kept licking but with more intent, pushing it in the direction of her teats. Eventually the lamb managed to stay standing up, legs splayed out in a desperate attempt at balance. The first few tottering steps took it close to the teat, but it carried on past in an uncontrolled rush, stuck its head up under her tail instead, and then fell over again.

This happened several times but at last, to my great relief, it found a teat. I could hear it sucking away noisily, but it didn't have long as Morag swung around and started straining again. Out popped lamb number two and the whole process was repeated.

By now I had a crick in my neck of epic proportions but I didn't care. I had never seen any creature being born before and was unprepared for the sense of wonder that came from the sight of those tiny lambs, so fragile, so vulnerable and yet in another way so tough, single-mindedly bent on survival. Within hours they were steady on their feet and able to run after their mother, which was just as well as Morag predictably took off across the field as soon as she saw me coming to pen her for the lambing checks.

With two ewes lambed safely and without any need of intervention by me, I started to feel more relaxed. My Jacobs were living up to their reputation for being wonderful mothers and, if Fatso and Missie delivered in the next few days, then life could go back to normal and I would be able to get a good night's sleep again, something I had previously taken for granted but now sorely missed.

But then nothing happened. Our lambing conveyor belt stalled. Missie and Fatso kept eating and getting bigger. Occasionally they would toy with me by sitting under a hedge or pawing the ground, but it never developed into anything. Unfortunately, the fact that nothing was happening didn't let me off the hook. My alarm still screeched at me in the early hours and I still had to plod down the lane to find them peaceful and calm and showing no signs of producing anything.

Two weeks later we finally had some progress, Missie with twins and Fatso with triplets. The fascinating thing about Fatso was that she didn't seem to look any thinner after giving birth. Her third lamb was much smaller than the other two and never caught up, not unusual with triplets as the bigger lambs always hog the teats, but they all muddled along happily enough together.

Despite my fears we had survived our first lambing season

and now had a thriving flock of twelve, eight lambs as well as our four ewes. I would lean against the gate on my way out for my evening walk with Lucy and feel a sense of pride as I watched the lambs racing each other along the hedge-line, pogoing into the air for the sheer joy of it, before turning about as one and racing back in the other direction. I didn't really have any right to feel proud as the sheep had done it all without me, but they were my flock and so I indulged myself. Lucy and I carried on through the village, which was bathed in that particular light that comes as the sun is setting, gold and mellow. I still missed Jessie, each walk lacking a presence with just one dog instead of two, but I took solace in thinking about those eight new lives in our field. As one door closes, another one opens. Nature redresses the balance and life goes on.

Chapter 8

Is it the winning that counts, or the taking part?

❖ ❖ ❖

'What do you think of these?'

With a flourish I placed a wicker basket on the table in front of Michael. Inside were three of my bantam eggs chosen, after much deliberation, for their perfect shape, colour and unblemished shells, nestling appealingly on a pale lilac napkin and decorated with a sprig of lavender picked from the garden.

Michael looked at them, then looked up at me before saying anything. I could see the cogs going round.

'They look very nice,' he said carefully.

'They look a lot more than nice. They look like the winning entry in the "Three eggs on a plate" competition.'

'Ah, but they're not on a plate. So that might be…'

'The winner last year put her eggs in a basket, not a plate. And so did several others.' I glared at him over the top of my glasses. 'If you can't beat them you join them so this year my eggs are in a basket.'

It was the first weekend in July which meant just one thing – the annual village show. The first show had taken place in 1988 which meant that the long-established families living in the village had a twenty-year history of vying for those coveted rosettes and certificates for first prize. Competition was fierce.

I left Michael fiddling about with a cake, his entry for the 'Men only home-made cake' competition and headed off to the village hall. All entries had to be signed in and displayed promptly first thing in the morning, after which the hall would briefly close for the judges to make their decisions, before reopening to the general public.

Despite it being a small village, there was precious little floor space left in the hall. Rows of tightly packed tables were laden with vegetables, fruits, cakes, flower decorations, artworks and photographs, a children's corner, chutneys, jams and wines – all home-grown or home-made and an inspiring testimony to the enduring traditions of rural life. These little shows took place all around the Black Mountains over the summer months, providing a time to relax and socialise with neighbours and friends as well as to win competitions.

I found the space on one of the tables that had my name on

it and arranged my basket of eggs to give them their best chance. Then I headed outside, making a beeline for the WI cake stall to buy my favourite fruit cake before they sold out. In our first year here I had been asked if I would like to contribute a cake to the stall. I politely explained that I'd never made a cake in my life, in fact that cooking wasn't really my thing, blissfully unaware that this wasn't the way to integrate myself into the community. Not only had I confirmed my doubtful status as an incomer who had no idea how village life worked, but I had also set myself apart as a woman who didn't cook. There was no doubting the fact that the ladies of the WI made wonderful cakes and any effort I might have made would have lowered their standards beyond redemption so they had in fact escaped lightly, but I don't think that helped.

With my fruit cake safely packed in my bag I wandered past the other stalls. The show took place on the same site each year (unless heavy rainfall and flooding stopped play), spread out over two fields that ran alongside a stream on the valley floor. I wandered past an assortment of stalls with old-fashioned games like 'Guess the weight' and a coconut shy. Dotted amongst them were tents promoting various farming and wildlife associations as well as the local sustainability group, and at the far end was a small marquee with a collection of old farming tools and vintage tractors. Time felt as if it had slowed, even gone backwards, a world away from the high-rise, high-pressure lifestyle of my marketing days. This show had stayed true to its roots so the theme was firmly agricultural and family orientated. There were no car boot stalls and no commercial fast-food sellers.

Crossing over the bridge I came to the second field, where the horse competitions took place. Two temporary showing rings had been marked out and the competitions had started already. A long line of horseboxes was parked up by the stream, with horses being backed down the ramps, hay nets hung up and water buckets put out, saddles, bridles and grooming kits being unpacked, hats and jackets donned. There were kids and their ponies, supremely confident despite the fact that some of them perched precariously in the saddle like tiny dolls, whilst the grown-ups sat proudly astride fine Welsh cobs or led stallions in hand. Many of these competitors were on their way to the Royal Welsh Show at Builth the following week, another reason that this blink-and-you-miss-it village show punched far above its weight in terms of both visitors and competitors.

Circling back into the main field, saving the best for last, I wandered through the livestock area, and eavesdropped shamelessly on the conversations around me as the farmers guided their sheep and cattle into the pens. There was an easy familiarity in their one-liners, their earthy humour and in their curt nods to each other. Farming people don't tend to waste words but I knew that many of these men had grown up together, gone to the same village school, learnt how to farm from their fathers and were now in charge of the family farm. There was a sense of continuity and knowing a person's history, good and bad. Their lines of connection were strongest in a historical sense, running back through time.

As incomers, our lines of connection ran in the opposite direction, running forwards, a future still to be made, relationships waiting to grow strong. We had no roots here, took people as we found them on first impressions and filled in the details as we got to know them better. As the farmers helped each other out, we and the other smallholders who had recently moved here also banded together, learning from each other as many of us had come to smallholding without generations of family to teach us what to do.

Like any society the village was made up of different groups, many of them overlapping with the same people: committees for the village hall, for the show, for the church, the regulars at the pub, including the old boys who played cards every Friday night and loved to take money off visitors from the campsite, the WI, the monthly book club meetings. It was a melting pot of faces familiar and new, young and old, from all walks of life.

Despite this diversity there was no doubt that it was the rural life that was the backbone, the framework that everything else revolved around. Even those who didn't farm or have animals themselves were probably close friends with, or related to, someone who did. No matter which way you turned, be it the track you walked along or the road you took to work each day, you were going to come across sheep or cattle or hay fields. In the background you would hear sheepdogs barking or a tractor chugging its way up the lane, a sheep trailer bouncing along behind it. Conversations in the pub might well cover all manner of subjects but you could guarantee that some discussion somewhere would be about the price of lamb or the never-ending mountain of paperwork that was an integral, much detested, part of modern farming.

This rural life defined and maintained the landscape and the animals that inhabited it. It also defined the people who lived in it, arranging them in an intricate web of relationships and beliefs, the centre of the web tightly packed and made up of the older, established families. We newcomers gathered on the outer edges, and whilst we were welcomed and included as part of the community, there was always a slight reserve that excluded us from those inner circles. I wondered how long it would take to lose the status of newcomer: at least a generation, or even longer in my case as I had a tendency to open my mouth and put my foot in it, which meant that we were never going to break through, but I understood that and was comfortable with it. Communities must evolve if they are to thrive; new blood is important and has a role to play. We would carve out our own place in this community over the coming years.

I was jolted out of my musing by the realisation that there

were no Jacob sheep in the pens, which didn't seem right. I flipped through my programme and there was definitely a category for them, but it seemed there were no entries. An image flashed into my mind of Timber winning 'Best ram' or one of my young ewe lambs parading around a ring with a rosette pinned to her halter. I resolved that the situation would be remedied next year and that some of my sheep would be in those pens.

Later that morning we waited anxiously for the results from the produce section of the show. At last the doors to the village hall were opened and there was a rush to see who would be taking a certificate back home to hang on the wall. I sidled up to my basket of eggs, preparing myself for disappointment. Each entry had a saucer next to it where they had cracked open an egg to check on its colour. It had to be a winner on the inside as well as on the outside. I looked and looked again. There it was! A glorious first place. I contented myself with the thought that I was slightly less of an incomer this afternoon than I had been earlier in the day and left to commiserate with Michael and his cake, which hadn't won a prize but still needed eating.

Later that year I booked myself onto a training day, run by the Jacob Sheep Society, which showed you how to prepare a sheep for the showing ring. I had already met the lady running the course, Brenda, as we had bought Morag and Fatso from her. She still referred to them by their fancy breed names and I never dared to tell her I had my own names for them. I might have got away with Morag, but calling a pedigree sheep by a name like Fatso probably wasn't the done thing. She was heavily involved in the Society, as well as breeding and showing her own flock, and I could understand that in such an environment the rules had to be adhered to.

She led out her chosen sheep for the demonstration on a halter. It followed meekly at her heels as she led it up a ramp and onto a platform where it could stand at a height that would allow her to work on it easily, rather than bending over for a couple of hours. She tied the halter rope to a metal ring and the sheep stood there, calm, patient and completely unfazed by the crowd of people standing around it.

From my own flock Morag had an excellent pedigree, and was a good-looking sheep, much more so than Fatso, so she would be the obvious candidate for entering into any competition, but words like meek, calm and patient weren't in her repertoire. I had tried a halter on her and she had bucked her way round the field, dragging me along with her.

Brenda explained that the process for preparing an animal for showing started weeks before the show. Sheep would be inspected so there was no point in even entering a sheep that was not up to the breed standards, which included things such as facial markings and comportment. That knocked Timber out straight away as he wasn't a pedigree and, whilst he was a superb specimen in my eyes, I knew his markings were all wrong. The sheep had to be trained to the halter to ensure that they walked and stood well which, barring a miracle, didn't bode well for showing Morag. Four to six weeks before the show the animal should be thoroughly washed and then allowed to dry naturally. Brenda had already given this sheep a shampoo, and indeed it did look squeaky clean in the manner of a 'one-that-I-prepared-earlier' example. I knew that if I washed any of my sheep they would be filthy again in a matter of hours and wondered how the showing fraternity kept the sheep clean over all those weeks.

The next stage entailed hours of brushing and fluffing up of the fleece. Those are my words; the correct term is to 'card' the fleece, which means to comb and untangle the wool fibres so that they all lie in the same direction. After that, out came the dagging shears which were used to trim the wool. The art was not in how much you cut off, but how much you left on, with the aim of making the sheep appear as wide and broad as possible. The carding and trimming process could be repeated as many as three times until you got a good 'face' on the wool.

By now the sheep was beginning to look bored, occasionally stamping its foot in protest, but its ordeal wasn't over yet. The feet had to be trimmed with clippers, the shape of the black markings around the face perfected with a small pair of scissors, unruly hairs around the ears were subdued, legs were washed and sprayed either black or white as the natural markings dictated to make them stand out further, and the final touch was a wool-fixing spray, a sheep version of hairspray, to ensure that the beautiful shape that you had just spent hours, if not days, creating, wouldn't be destroyed once the sheep decided it had an itch that needed a good rubbing on the nearest fence post.

By now the sheep had definitely had enough and so had the audience. It was time for a lunch break. Brenda and her husband had prepared us a salad lunch with fresh produce from her garden and as I sat there wishing my home-grown Cos lettuce looked and tasted this good, I realised that English was the minority language in this group. The course was being held in west Wales, not far from Newcastle Emlyn, where the Welsh language was still spoken by many people, far more than it was around Crickhowell where we lived. It wasn't just the older generation who were here to learn either: the participants on this course were a mixture of all ages, and it was heartening to see a number of young teenagers, both male and female, who worked on the family farm and had an appetite for showing their own livestock.

It was just as well they were keen to do it and could keep the traditions alive, because I had a suspicion that this wasn't for me. We spent the afternoon practising what Brenda had shown us in the morning session and after a couple of hours I knew beyond doubt that no amount of training and patience would turn Morag into a beast who would submit to all this pampering and fussing. Even if I could train up one of her offspring from a lamb, it still wasn't something that I felt motivated to do. I never spent any time on brushing and blow-drying my own hair, rarely wore make-up or fancy clothes, and it seemed counterintuitive to spend hours and hours preparing a humble sheep for the farming version of the catwalk.

The next year when the village show came around I made a beeline for the sheep pens. This time there were a couple of Jacobs in the pens, although they weren't mine. I cast a critical and knowing eye over them, a little knowledge ever being a dangerous thing, and contented myself with the thought that if I had entered any of my sheep, we would have won hands down. That was good enough for me.

Chapter 9

Full circle

❖ ❖ ❖

'How am I supposed to choose?'

This was a rhetorical question as I was alone and the only person who could answer that question was me. I leant on the gate to the sheep field, casting a proprietary eye over my first batch of lambs as they grazed peacefully under a weak winter sun. They were seven months old now, three tups, five ewes, and they looked well. Tomorrow afternoon we would load up four of them and take them to the abattoir. I had to choose which four to keep and which four would go, providing us and some of our neighbours and friends with meat for the winter.

I had always known this moment was coming and on one level I was comfortable with it. These lambs had enjoyed a good life, had been raised naturally without antibiotics or medications and, if I was going to eat meat at all, I would rather do it this way than pick up a packet from the supermarket shelf with no idea of what life that animal had led, or what it might have in its bloodstream that would then enter into my own body.

It wasn't just a question of a good life, there was also the issue of a good death, if there can ever be such a thing. We were lucky enough to have a small, family-run abattoir twenty minutes' drive away. Three generations of the family had worked in this business and all the local farmers used them. They had a good reputation and reputations needed to be upheld in rural communities. The usual procedure was to deliver the sheep the day before they were due to be killed which would give them the night to settle in and calm down in their new surroundings. This is done for two reasons, one a consequence of the other. The first reason is to minimise the stress to the animal. Secondly, an animal that is frightened releases adrenaline, which in turn uses up glycogen and this can affect the taste of the meat, making it tougher, lacking in taste and high in acidity.

In the 1930s there were 30,000 abattoirs in the UK. By 2019 that number had dropped to 250 with 32 large-scale abattoirs in England slaughtering 88% of sheep. I can't imagine what such an enterprise would look like or how it would feel to work there, although I am pretty sure it would put me off eating meat for life.[3] In Wales we had 26 abattoirs, two of them less than half an hour away and both of which were family-run businesses set up for small numbers of sheep.

It is one thing to be comfortable with a principle, and quite another to put it into practice, especially for the first time, and part of me was dreading tomorrow. I turned away from the gate and headed home. I already knew which lambs would be leaving us so standing there prevaricating wouldn't change anything. I had some paperwork to do.

As with anything in life, running a smallholding involves administration. The paperwork trail started from the day we took on our smallholding, and came full circle today as I spent the evening filling in the necessary forms for our visit to the abattoir tomorrow. A word of warning to anyone who is tempted to follow in our footsteps: you'll have to get used to abbreviations. Step one is to register the holding by applying for a County Parish Holding (CPH). You don't need to own the land to do this and it costs nothing. Its purpose is to enable the authorities to track the location and movement of stock in order to prevent and control disease.

To move up the ladder to the next step we contacted the

---

[3] 'The future of small abattoirs in the UK', NFU Cymru, https://www.nfu-cymru.org.uk/

Animal and Plant Health Agency (APHA) to obtain our flock number. This number is printed on ear tags, without which we would not legally be allowed to move our sheep from the property.

Record keeping came next, with a flock book in which we recorded all details of our animals, and an annual inventory form that provided a record of the number of animals on the holding at the same date each year.

If we wanted to move our sheep anywhere, be it to a show, to pick up a new ewe or ram, go to an auction or the abattoir, we had to fill in a movement form which came in triplicate, one for the sheep owner, one for the abattoir in this case and one to be sent in to the relevant authority.

Lastly, there was the Food Chain Information form (FCI) with tick boxes to confirm that the medical withdrawal periods had been adhered to and to provide details of any disease.

We set off the next day with the relevant paperwork and four lambs in the sheep trailer. This was the culmination of a year's work but both of us were subdued and in a way I was glad. Taking a life should never be done flippantly or without an awareness of what you are doing. If we ever got to the stage where a journey like this meant nothing to us then I fear we would have lost some vital element of our respect for the animals we cared for.

The entrance to the abattoir was through a public car park in the village. We arrived to find ourselves in a queue of trailers, some with sheep, some with pigs. The off-loading process was quick and efficient; each trailer swung round to a gate, the animals were funnelled into a series of pens in some rather ancient looking sheds and then the driver reversed out, a tricky manoeuvre which required good handling skills and which was why Michael was driving and not me. While he parked up in the car park I went in search of the office, my paperwork in my hand.

It wasn't immediately clear where I should go. I asked the lad dealing with the next trailer and he pointed vaguely to the back of the house which was attached to the sheds. I walked down a narrow alleyway past what I assumed to be the abattoir itself, trying not to look at a huge bin full of skinned sheep fleeces, and found myself with a choice of doors to go through. Luckily for me, one opened and I recognised the farmer who had been in the queue ahead of us.

'Just through there, love.' He gestured behind him. 'They'll soon sort you out.'

I nodded my thanks and walked into what seemed to be a kitchen, similar to one that you would find in any house. There was a young lad sitting at the table with a stack of forms in front of him, and an older man sitting at the other end of the table drinking a cup of tea and reading a newspaper. He looked up, smiled at me briefly, then returned to his reading.

The lad held out a hand for my paperwork, and as he raised his head I could see the family resemblance between him and the older man, obviously his father. He ticked off various boxes, scribbled in dates and times, and stacked the various copies into piles with a speed which showed he had done this many times before.

'They'll be ready in a couple of days. Do you want the offal?'

I nodded.

And that was it. I was aware that someone else had come in behind me and was waiting to pass on his paperwork, and so I turned and left. I could hear the sound of conversation behind me, on a first-name basis, and wondered how many times I would have to visit before they would speak to me with such familiarity. I walked back along the line of waiting trailers, now petering out, feeling as if I was on as much of a conveyor belt as the sheep were. One trailer in, another one out. One human in, another one out. There was no time for standing around feeling maudlin.

'So how was it?' asked Michael as I climbed back into the Land Rover.

'Quick,' I replied.

'Are you all right?'

'I think so.'

As we drove home I tried to put myself in the shoes of the men who worked in the abattoir, tried to imagine how it must feel to spend so many hours of your day stunning and killing animals and then cutting them up, hosing down the floors and collecting the blood for use in pet products or as a form of dried fertiliser. Living animals in, carcasses out, a sentient being that was turned into a lump of meat. This family also had their own butcher's shop, fronting onto the high street, so they would be completely familiar with the act of processing meat, turning it into chops and joints, the smell of it in their noses every day. It was their livelihood, their business, and they didn't have the luxury of getting sentimental about what they were doing.

Neither did I, although it wasn't easy. I had to accept this as part of the process or stop eating meat altogether which wasn't something I felt ready to do. Every creature on this earth is part of a food chain and, in my opinion, eating meat is a natural thing to do. What is not at all natural is to treat animals as a commodity, strip them of all their natural habits and confine them in battery farms or sheds where they never see the light of day. What mattered to us was that we knew our animals had lived as natural a life as possible and had been well cared for. When we ate meat that we had not produced ourselves we chose free-range, often from the local butcher's shop, where they took care and pride in sourcing from local free-range flocks and herds. We paid more for it, but we balanced this out by buying a little less and eating more vegetables.

A few days later our lambs arrived back in four boxes, now a mixture of different cuts of meat: shoulders, racks, legs and chops, neck, kidneys and shanks all vacuum-packed and ready to be distributed to friends and family who had placed orders with us. Our aim was to try to cover our costs by selling off two of the lambs and keeping the other two for ourselves. We laid the contents of two of the boxes out on the table and felt overwhelmed at the amount of meat we had, but then came the first knock at the door, our neighbour dropping in to pick up their order. A few hours later, a few more knocks at the door, and suddenly there was nothing left.

'I hope it tastes all right,' I said nervously as I put a shoulder of lamb in the oven for our evening meal. 'If not, nobody will buy anything from us next year.'

Later that evening we sat down to our first home-reared roast lamb. I raised my glass to Michael, and in my head I gave a silent thank you to the lamb, and then took a mouthful of the most succulent, most delicious lamb I had ever tasted. I might have been biased of course, but if I was I really didn't mind. We had come full circle, from tupping in the previous autumn, to lambing in the spring and, finally, to eating our own meat this winter. These cycles would become the way we measured our year, and with each revolution I hoped we would become more experienced and more at ease with the challenges that this lifestyle would bring.

Chapter 10

Grow your own

❖ ❖ ❖

'Do we really need this many vegetable beds?' I leaned on my spade and rubbed my aching back.

'Given that you've ordered enough seeds to feed the village, yes, we do,' said Michael.

I couldn't think of a suitable answer to this as I lose any sense of moderation as soon as I open a seed catalogue. I wondered if the marketing department in these companies spent a fortune on consumer research because they have certainly perfected the art of timing, knowing exactly when to send them out for maximum effect. It's the depth of winter, the weather is relentless, I'm at my lowest ebb and that's when I hear a promising, heavy thud as the post lands on the mat. My day becomes brighter from the first page and keeps getting better as

I work my way through to the back cover, trying not to swoon at pictures of impossibly lush courgettes, or beautifully arranged peppers, and tomatoes in summer shades of red, orange and yellow. Leeks and potatoes may not seem the most exciting of vegetables but once combined in a soup they add up to far more than the sum of the parts. Slender, perfectly shaped carrots in shades of yellow, purple and orange compete with exotic squashes and plump melons. As my 'must have' list grows ever longer, a little voice inside reminds me that my vegetables didn't look this good last year, or the year before, but that is beside the point.

This chunky booklet, which seemed to get bigger each year, was so much more than just a selection of vegetables: it represented hope, the promise of a new season and an end to winter. Who could resist such a thing? Certainly not me.

However, standing on the side of the hill with a chilly winter wind turning my nose and cheeks red, struggling to create a vegetable allotment out of a field full of couch grass and stones, the promise of a bountiful harvest seemed a very long way away.

After several days of hard graft we had eight large beds, all neatly turned over and ready for planting in the spring. The next job was to fence it off, an even bigger job in some ways as we needed to keep the rabbits out. We dug a trench along the fence lines and buried the wire netting underneath it. The last job was a small fruit cage for our fruit bushes.

We soon learned that we were better at raising animals than we were at raising vegetables. It shames me to admit it, but we simply didn't put in the time needed to grow vegetables on this scale. They grew well enough, but we couldn't keep on top of the weeding and we were frankly hopeless at harvesting, particularly crops like broccoli which go over so quickly. This is not to say that we didn't have our successes because we did, particularly in our first year when we had a spring and summer full of sunshine and everything flourished, but our results fell far short of self-sufficiency.

Our efforts at procuring our own food were not limited to the allotment. We also experimented with what the natural world had to offer. As a birthday present one year I bought Michael a weekend on a mushroom foraging course, and although it was technically his present it seemed only right that I would go along as well. We spent the day rifling through the leaf mould in the wooded hillsides of the Elan Valley and took our bounty back to the hotel in the evening where it was served up as a mushroom-tasting event. The majority of them fell into the 'do-it-once-but-not-again' category but parasol mushrooms gently fried in butter and a slice of a giant puffball with a goose egg on top of it proved to be delicious and we developed the habit of keeping an eye out for these particular mushrooms on our walks.

The steep sides of the reservoirs around the Elan Valley also provided rich pickings for bilberries. We would pick as we walked, enjoying the explosion of flavour in our mouths, but the berries were so tiny we never had the patience necessary to pick a substantial quantity. This activity always brought back bittersweet memories of Jessie, as she had enjoyed them even more than we did, bulldozing her way through the carpet of dense low-growing bushes and deftly picking off the berries with her teeth.

Another weekend we joined a different foraging course, this time for edible plants. With our guide pointing us in the right direction we ambled through meadows picking out sorrel, wild garlic, meadowsweet, wild chervil and burdock, none of which we would be able to remember when we got home. We expended more energy picking our leaves than we gained from eating them but it was a pleasant day out.

We were far more successful with home-made wine and beer. Michael began with home-brew kits but soon graduated to putting his own ingredients together, sourcing malted barley, hops and yeast and devoting most of a day to the process, steeping and mashing until the kitchen smelt like a brewery. Each batch provided us with twenty-five litres of very drinkable beer. We would offer it to friends and neighbours, note the slightly wary look that came across their faces at the word 'home-brew', and see it change to appreciation as they took that first tentative sip. The barrel never lasted long.

Producing consistently good home-made wines was not so easy. Our favourite was blackberry wine, picked from the hedgerows, but it was a complete lottery as to whether it would be good, bad or indifferent. Our first year was average, but on our second year we picked the berries whilst on a camping trip near the Elan Valley in mid-Wales and the result was like nectar, rich and smooth, and better than many shop-bought wines. We picked from the same spot the following year, followed all the same procedures and it didn't come anywhere close, average at best. Another time we experimented with some home-grown parsnips and the result was undrinkable. Elderflower champagne worked well apart from the unfortunate side-effect of giving everybody wind.

As the berries ripened and autumn rolled in we began making jams and chutneys. I am not a great cook and don't find time spent at the stove to be a soothing experience, but there was something calming about making chutney, watching our large preserving pan bubbling away with a heady concoction of fruit and spices. In the new year, once the Seville oranges were on sale, we turned our attention to marmalade.

We ended up with so many jars, pots and bottles of produce that there wasn't enough room for them all in the kitchen cupboards. We built a shelving system down in the garage, squeezing it in next to our chest freezer, and it gave me great satisfaction to see the results of all our hard work, jars and bottles neatly labelled and stacked, strings of onions hanging from the ceiling and a freezer full of meat and vegetables. It was good to know that the primal human instinct of the hunter-gatherer hadn't been completely overwhelmed by a lifetime of visits to the supermarket. If the world came to an end we wouldn't starve, although we might get a bit bored with rhubarb and orange chutney.

This particular element of our smallholding life taught us the sobering lesson of just how difficult it is to be totally self-sufficient. It requires a huge commitment in terms of time, energy and organisation, recognising that there will be certain times of the year when it completely takes you over. Nothing can be taken for granted. If you have a bumper harvest of fruit one year, the next is likely to be poor. The weather takes a pernicious delight in ruining a crop you have been nurturing for months, the wasps and birds will nibble their way through your apples and pears, the mice and squirrels will munch their way through anything they can get despite all the obstacles you put in their way. Then there are the events you can't foresee, one example in our case being the cattle in the adjoining field escaping, barging their way through our painstakingly erected fencing and trampling all over the vegetables. It can be as much a thankless task as a deeply satisfying one and we never knew which way the balance might swing.

Over the years we learnt to accept the rough with the smooth but at some point we decided that the goal of being completely self-sufficient in growing our own fruit and vegetables made life harder than we needed it to be. We would accept the bounty of each year for what it was, and be grateful that we could fall back on local veggie schemes and an excellent greengrocer in our nearest town when we needed to.

Of course, none of this diminished the excitement of the seed catalogues arriving in the post each year. And I never managed to rein in my enthusiasm and order just what I needed, allowing myself instead to be seduced by a mixture of weird and wonderful varieties that invariably failed for one reason or another. I blame it on the marketing department. Long may they continue.

Chapter 11

Wedding

❖ ❖ ❖

'Do you fancy getting married?' asked Michael.

I looked at him. 'Could do.'

Some decisions are very easy.

We had both been married before, Michael in the church in the same village where we now lived, with a horse-drawn carriage and a big reception at a nearby hotel. I had been married in a registrar's office, with the reception in a hotel in Surrey. I had memories of a harpist serenading the guests and of myself wearing a cream dress, looking like a puffed-up meringue, and had no desire to repeat the experience. In fact, for some reason that seems slightly odd to me now, this time round I wanted to get married in my walking boots and shorts, which was taking it from one extreme to the other.

We both wanted a quiet wedding, a small affair with no fuss. The cost of having a big wedding seemed completely crazy to us, a fortune spent in one day. We'd rather spend the money on a good holiday, or the honeymoon, and from there was born the idea that we would get married in Tasmania and combine it with a trip to Australia, something we had long wanted to do.

We were aware that this was going to be a plane journey too far for friends and family and that there would be considerable disappointment that we were taking ourselves so far away to tie the knot. It wasn't that we didn't want to share this happy event with our loved ones, but we both felt uncomfortable being the centre of so much attention for a day and we preferred to do something different. Our solution was to book a holiday cottage in the Brecon Beacons for a week on our return. It had space for twelve people at any one time and we organised it so that we had a steady stream of family and friends coming and going over the week. We could spend quality time with small groups of people and celebrate our marriage with them belatedly. The only proviso was that everyone helped with the cooking!

The other big issue was what to do about all our animals. Nowadays it would be easy, with online organisations like TrustedHousesitters offering a ready supply of people keen to come and stay for free in your house and in return keep an eye on both the property and any animals that came with it. Back then, we knew we would have to pay for this service. By pure coincidence I spotted an advert in the local vets for a new house-sitting business. An enterprising young woman had just started it up and agreed to take us on. It was January, a quiet time in the smallholding year, and we hoped that keeping an eye on our menagerie would be relatively straightforward. I left her with contact numbers if she needed help, backed up by endless lists of 'what to do if...' and we set off on our travels.

Things had changed since my first marriage, when the only alternative to a church was a registry office. Now, all sorts of places had licences which allowed them to perform marriage ceremonies and in Tasmania you could do it anywhere you liked, as long as you had the ceremony officiated by a registered celebrant. We met our celebrant, a lady called Gail, for lunch at a quayside bar on the harbour in Hobart, the capital of Tasmania. We sat out in the sunshine, sipping a glass of champagne to celebrate the occasion, and discussed how our marriage day would unfold.

We wanted to get married outside, and had chosen the location based on some photos we had seen of the cliffs around Pirates Bay, about an hour's drive from Hobart. Gail knew the area and had drawn us a map to a place that might be suitable for a small group of people to hold a ceremony. We would look at it later that afternoon on the way to our B&B. She had also arranged for her husband, and the wife of the person her husband worked for, to be our witnesses. Afterwards we would all return to our

B&B for a simple lunch. It seemed very straightforward.

Driving up to the cliffs we found a small gravelled area, parked the car, and put on our walking boots.

'Hmm,' said Michael as he read Gail's notes on the spot she had suggested for the ceremony. 'I'm not sure you're going to approve.'

'Why?'

'This is it.' He waved his arm around the car park. 'This is where we can get married.'

'But it's a car park.'

'She did say there weren't many options. Looking at the map, I think she may be right.'

'I am not getting married in a car park. Let's walk further along the cliff path. I'm sure we can find something better than this.'

The problem with cliff paths is that they can be very narrow, and very precipitous. This particular trail hugged the contours of the cliffs and was barely wide enough for one person. A low-growing, dense scrub carpeted the ground on the landward side, with a sheer drop down to the water on the other.

'How about this?' Michael had found a place where the path widened slightly, now big enough for two people to stand abreast. I inched up to him, looked tentatively over the edge and immediately stepped back.

'We can't fit five people in this tiny space. And if one of us steps in the wrong direction it'll turn into a funeral rather than a wedding.'

'I like it.'

'Well I don't.'

We spent another hour tramping up and down the path in both directions, becoming progressively more depressed and irritable as the time passed.

'I can't do this any more,' I said eventually. 'Let's go and book in to our accommodation, have a cup of tea and a rest and then decide what to do.'

'We're getting married tomorrow morning. We haven't exactly got much time to…'

'I know that.' I glared at him. 'But I need a cup of tea and a sit down. I'm exhausted.'

Our B&B was at a place called Osprey Lodge in the village of Eaglehawk Neck. It was set slightly back from the waterfront, overlooking the cobalt-blue waters of Pirates Bay. From the pictures that we found on the internet when we booked it, it looked like a slice of paradise. Reality didn't disappoint. As our host led us along the path to the self-contained cabin that would be our home for the next few days, I could feel all the stress of the last hour fading away. She showed us in and then hovered by the door.

'Oh,' I said.

A magnificent bouquet of flowers stood on the table, with

half a dozen bottles of champagne around it, each one decorated with ribbons and a card from the sender. A pile of wedding cards sat on the table next to them.

'Oh,' I said again.

'We feel like we know most of your family and friends,' said our host with a smile. 'They sent us some money for the flowers and the champagne and we've had cards arriving all week. One of them is a voucher so that you can go out for a meal as well. It's a good restaurant, we know it well. I hope it's all ok?'

I nodded. It's not often words fail me but I could feel myself welling up and didn't dare speak for fear I'd start blubbing. There were times when I had wondered if we'd made the right decision to take ourselves so far away from everybody we loved for this marriage, but right now it felt as if they were all here in this little cabin with us. The sense of love was overwhelming.

'It's wonderful,' I managed eventually, my voice slightly wobbly. 'Thank you so much.'

Once she'd gone Michael came over and gave me a hug.

'You're not going to go all emotional on me, are you?'

'I might.' I stuck my nose in the flowers and sniffed. 'I never expected this. It's just amazing. So kind. So thoughtful.'

After discussions with both the B&B owners and our celebrant about where we should hold the ceremony a plan eventually emerged, albeit a different one than we had initially hoped for. Despite our blue skies that evening, the weather forecast for the next morning was for heavy rainfall, another nail in the coffin for a cliffside ceremony and my wedding outfit of boots and shorts.

In the end we still got married outside but, as the promised rain did indeed arrive, we held the ceremony under cover of an arbour in the beautiful gardens that surrounded our cabin.

'What are you going to wear?' asked Michael that morning, in a deceptively casual tone. 'Given that we're not out on the cliff path any more.'

'Are you saying that you don't want to get married to me if I'm wearing muddy boots and an old pair of shorts?'

'I'd marry you if you wore a dustbin liner, but you look so much prettier in a dress.'

I sighed. I did have a dress. And some shoes. I'd bought them under duress whilst we were visiting Michael's family in Adelaide the previous week, but I had still hoped to wear my boots. Now that we had changed the venue, they didn't seem quite the right thing any more.

'And we're only going to do this once.' He pulled the dress out of the wardrobe and held it against himself. 'It's a lovely dress. Very you. Shame not to use it.'

And so I got married in a dress and new shoes that hurt my feet, but it was still a magical day.

Afterwards we shared a buffet lunch of lobster freshly caught from the bay with the strangers who had shared our wedding day. This was another point when I had wondered if I would miss our family and friends, and in one way I certainly did. However it still felt good to be spending the day with this small group of people who had made us feel so welcome, and who had gone out of their way to make our day special. They might appear only briefly in our lives but they would not be forgotten.

After lunch, once everybody had left, the dress went back in the wardrobe, and my grateful feet slid back into their walking boots. We grabbed our waterproof jackets and went out for a walk. The grey clouds rolled away on a high breeze and the sun came out. I have a photo of us from that afternoon, our trousers rolled up to our knees, our boots tied together and slung around our shoulders, as we waded barefoot through clear blue waters on a sandy beach.

Weddings don't get any better than that.

Part 2

Settling in

Chapter 12

New faces

❖ ❖ ❖

'I think we need another dog.' I looked at Lucy, curled up in her basket next to the Rayburn. 'I think Lucy would like the company.'

'Maybe Lucy is happy with how things are now. She gets all the attention,' said Michael.

'Well, maybe *I* would like another dog then.'

Michael hitched up his rucksack. 'We haven't got time to discuss this now. Can it wait until I get back?'

I nodded. 'Have you got everything?'

'Yup.'

'Have you got the directions of where you're going?'

'Nope.'

For his birthday present I had bought him a weekend course

on tree-climbing. I'm not sure why I did this, as the thought of him swinging around in the tree tops made me think of broken legs and worse, but I knew it was something he wanted to do.

'Have a good time and please be careful.' I gave him a hug.

'Promise me you won't do anything rash.' He tried to give me a stern look.

'About what?'

'You know what. No puppies. At least not until we talk about it and I have more time to get used to the idea.'

'All right. But there's no harm in thinking about it.'

I waved him off, took Lucy out for a walk around the village and tried not to think about getting another dog. I had assumed that the hole that Jessie left behind when she died would get smaller over time. That didn't seem to be happening. Instead, so many things went out of their way to remind me that she was gone. Even walking with Lucy felt wrong. I was so used to having two dogs.

It wasn't just about the number of dogs, it was also about the character of the dog. Lucy was the sweetest of creatures, as long as she wasn't on a lead with other dogs around, but once in the house she tended to go to her basket and stay there. She was so quiet it was almost as if she didn't exist, whereas Jessie had been a constant presence, a real companion. And that special bond was what I was missing more than anything.

Back at home I went over to the dresser and pulled out a

scrap of paper on which I had scrawled a telephone number and the name of a farmer the other side of Abergavenny who had a litter for sale. I had been given these contact details a couple of weeks ago by a friend who knew I was beginning to think it was time for another dog. I sighed and put it away. I couldn't do anything until I had talked it over with Michael.

I had plenty of things to occupy me that day. The Studio needed to be prepared for the next set of guests and the henhouse needed a fresh coat of paint but always at the back of my mind I kept thinking about that slip of paper in the drawer. What harm could it do to just give them a call? It was highly likely that all the puppies had gone by now, and then I could put it out of my mind. By the late afternoon I had convinced myself that this was the only sensible course of action if I didn't want to drive myself crazy.

There were two puppies left, a boy and a girl. The farmer's wife said I could come up the following morning and have a look and, before I could stop myself, I had agreed. I am convinced that there is another person inside my head, a sly creature who bides her time and then leaps in and commits me to things that I should have left well alone. I know she is there, and yet so often she still takes me by surprise.

As I drove to the farm the next morning, I gave myself a stiff talking-to. I was only going to look. If I wanted to take it any further then it could wait until Michael came back and we could arrange another visit together. I pulled up in the yard, knocked on the door and the farmer's wife took me round the back to a dilapidated shed. There were four puppies inside.

'What happened to the mother?' I asked, noting how dark the shed was, and the lack of any form of bedding. It didn't smell too good either.

'Out working the sheep. She'll be along later.' The woman bent down and picked up two of the pups by the scruff of their necks. 'These are the two that are still available. Nine weeks old now. Did you want a bitch or a dog?'

'Female.'

She handed me a little scrap of brown fur. I had been told that the litter had a mixed parentage, part collie, part springer, but it looked like the springer genes had come out on top with this one. She was an odd looking creature, and looking at her a French word sprung to mind, *jolie-laide*, which means both ugly and pretty at the same time. She was both these things, depending on which way you looked at her. Her coat was mainly a rich chestnut colour with a bit of mottled white fur around her neck and down her chest. She had long, soft spaniel ears and the fur between them was wildly curly but the rest of her coat was smooth. Something banged loudly out in the yard, a heavy metal door swinging shut in the wind, and she cringed against me.

'Very timid, that one,' said the farmer's wife, dismissively. 'You'd probably do better with the dog.'

It was true the male puppy seemed much more outgoing. He was down on the ground chewing at my boot laces with more force than seemed possible from such a small being. The puppy in my arms wriggled, pushed her nose against my neck and gave me a lick. I could feel the warmth of her little body against mine and knew I was lost.

And so I left with a new puppy. And with each mile that took me closer to home the sense of guilt grew stronger, until I could almost imagine it as an accusing presence sitting on the seat next to me. This wasn't how Michael and I did things. We were a team; we made decisions together. He'd be back in a few hours. How was I going to tell him?

The process of getting the puppy settled in distracted me for an hour or so. Once she was a bit bigger she could have Jessie's old bed, but for now she needed something smaller so I pulled out a cardboard box and lined it with one of my old fleeces as a temporary measure. Then I covered the kitchen floor with newspaper, sighing as I remembered the joys of toilet training.

Lucy was decidedly unimpressed, taking one sniff and then retiring to her bed. When the puppy teetered towards her as part of her exploration of this strange new home, which must have seemed very different after being confined in a shed for most of her young life, Lucy curled her lip and growled, sending the youngster running in the opposite direction. She certainly was of a nervous disposition, but I knew they would get used to each other in a few days.

The thought of how I would tell Michael about our new arrival weighed ever heavier on my mind as the afternoon progressed. I kept an ear out for the sound of the Land Rover so I could catch him before he came into the kitchen and saw my evil deed for himself, but I didn't get down the stairs quick enough and missed my chance. I skidded into the kitchen, saw him standing in the doorway with a bemused expression on his face, and braced myself.

'So who is this?' He came further into the room, his eyes fixed on the puppy, who cowered down into her bed, obviously unsure about the new man in her life.

'I haven't given her a name yet,' I said, warily. 'It all happened too quickly.'

'Did I imagine a conversation we had about waiting until I came back before we got a new dog?'

'No, you didn't, but…'

'And did I imagine that you promised you wouldn't do anything rash?'

'I'm sorry. I really am.' My guilty confession poured out of me, as I explained that I really was only going to look and never meant to come back with a puppy. 'I don't know how it happened,' I ended, realising how lame that sounded.

'I can't say I'm that surprised.' He sighed in exasperation.

'Does that mean you forgive me?'

'No, it just means that I know you very well. Better than you know yourself by the look of it.' He cocked his head on one side. 'She's a funny looking little thing.'

Something in his tone must have given the puppy some encouragement. She scrambled out of her box, and then grovelled her way over to him, her belly so low it scraped along the floor. She looked up at him, this new human towering over her, and her tail started to wag, just a tentative, testing-the-waters sort of waggle to begin with and then one where her whole body joined in. She put her front paws on Michael's boots and he bent down to pick her up.

I started to breathe again. She would work her puppy magic on him and everything would be alright. And then the excitement all got too much for her and she peed. All the way down his jacket. A little trickle of puppy pee goes a surprisingly long way. There are times when there is nothing you can say to make things better.

We called her Maddie. She remained scared of most things for the rest of her life, but she loved people and, even as an older dog, would wiggle her way ecstatically towards complete strangers, her whole body wagging in time with her tail.

❖❖❖

Maddie wasn't our only new arrival that year. A farmer down the valley who normally bought and sold horses and ponies had fallen prey to an impulse buy and bought a donkey at a horse sale. At the time he had thought it might be a good investment as donkeys were becoming popular but it turned out to be a fad that faded away as quickly as it started and now he had a female donkey that he didn't really need.

Unlike horses and ponies, donkeys' coats are not naturally waterproof, which puts them at a definite disadvantage with our wet Welsh weather. They need a shelter, which this donkey didn't have as the farmer kept his horses out all year. We had a shelter and he had heard that we wanted a companion for Snari. If we wanted to take the donkey on loan then he was happy to bring it over in a trailer.

Snari had spent the first six years of his life in Iceland and Michael had bought him eight years ago from the person who had first imported him. He'd probably never seen a donkey before so it would be interesting to see how they reacted to each other. He was a very easy-going, placid character so we didn't foresee any problems.

The minute she set foot in the field his whole demeanour changed. It was as if someone had flicked a switch. His head came up, his neck arched and he high-stepped his way over to her in a way we'd never seen before. It was as if the years of domestication disappeared in an instant, allowing his wild, proud heritage to break free. He looked magnificent.

'Wow,' breathed Michael. 'I've never seen him look like that.'

'He's behaving like a stallion. But he's gelded.' I watched as Snari sidled up to the donkey, snaking his head from side to side with an unmistakeable intention behind it. 'He *is* gelded, isn't he?'

Michael nodded.

The donkey didn't seem as impressed as we were with Snari's display of virility. He tried to bite her neck and she swung round and whacked him hard in the chest with both back feet. We could hear the thud from where we stood at the gate. Undeterred, he came in again from a different direction, and then again, and each time she saw him off in no uncertain terms.

'Poor Snari,' said Michael.

'Attagirl,' I said. 'You show him what's what.'

Eventually Snari realised that nothing was going to come of it and the fire faded out of him. They retreated to separate ends of the field, each keeping a watchful eye on the other. Over time they became good friends, shadowing each other as they grazed and even indulging in mutual grooming.

Apparently the donkey had come from a family who had called her Wonky. We tried to imagine ourselves calling this word out across the field to bring her in and decided we couldn't do it. Instead we called her Bella, because she was beautiful – in a donkey sort of way.

Chapter 13

Getting along with pigs

❖ ❖ ❖

Historically mankind has had a long and close relationship with pigs. It wasn't that long ago that many households had one out in the backyard, feeding it scraps during the year and then killing it to provide meat for the family over Christmas and beyond. How quickly things change. In modern times we rarely see a live pig. The vast majority of them are shut away and farmed intensively. When something is out of sight, it's out of mind, but the more deeply we became involved in our smallholding life, the harder it was to turn a blind eye to the realities of modern livestock farming. In many cases it had become industrialised to the point where the animals might just as well have been nuts and bolts on a factory floor, rather than sentient beings who felt fear and pain, who needed companionship and a sense of belonging with their own kind just as we did.

With regard to pigs in particular, this situation wasn't helped by the fact that they were victims of an often undeserved reputation for attributes that weren't particularly endearing. Phrases like 'your bedroom looks like a pigsty', 'sweating like a pig' or calling someone a pig because they are greedy or overweight have been part of everyday speech for years and yet they don't give a fair representation of a pig. If pigs are allowed to roam freely, as they would in a natural habitat, they are fastidious creatures and will not defecate in the place they eat or sleep. Young piglets will begin this practice within five days of being born. Neither do pigs sweat, as they have very few sweat glands. They roll around in mud or water as a means of keeping cool. Studies have shown that they are as intelligent, sociable and affectionate as any dog, yet we eat one and love the other. The unfortunate pig drew the short straw in that contest.[4]

It is true that they will eat practically anything and this has led to an association with 'being unclean' in parts of the world. There are numerous gory stories of them eating human remains, one example being the tale of a farmer in Oregon who had a heart attack and fell into the pig enclosure. He didn't come out again.

Given how we felt about trying to eat meat from an animal

---

[4] 'Swine smarts – are pigs really intelligent animals?', https://thehumaneleague.org/article/pig-intelligence, March 15th 2022

that had been raised as naturally as possible, it was inevitable that there would come a day when we decided to have our own pigs and with that came the usual research into what type of pig we should get, where we would keep them and whether this was a long-term commitment to breeding or whether to keep it simple and buy in some young weaners.

We spent time talking to other smallholders who had pigs, as well as pig breeders, and finally decided upon the Berkshire as our chosen breed. Also known as 'the Lady's pig', it had the reputation of being friendly, hardy and suited to outdoor living, not too big and so not too intimidating for first-timers as well as providing very tasty meat.

The Berkshire is a black pig, with white feet, and is one of the UK's oldest breeds, dating back to the seventeenth century.[5] It is also referred to as the 'Royal Berkshire' due to the Royal family keeping a herd at Windsor for hundreds of years. If I were to use the correct term, a group of pigs isn't referred to as a herd at all, but as a 'drift' or a 'drove'.

---

[5] British Pig Association, https://britishpigs.org.uk/berkshire

As we were new to keeping pigs, we decided to ease ourselves in and buy three weaners, aged around eight weeks old, and keep them for approximately six months or so until they reached a good weight. From what we could gather they were much easier to look after than sheep, needing far less attention and being much more robust.

We sectioned off a large area in one of our rented fields, erected some sturdy fencing around it and built our own pig ark. We promised the landowner half a pig as payment and with the proviso that we would make the land good and return it to how it had been once the pigs had finished wrecking it.

And so came the day when we let our three little piglets out of the trailer and into their new home.

'What shall we call them?' I asked.

'Perhaps we shouldn't give them names, given that they'll only be with us for six months and then we'll eat them,' said

Michael.

'It hasn't stopped us with the lambs,' I replied. 'And we need to know who is who in case one gets ill or something. They all look the same to me though.'

We watched them for a while as they explored their territory, snuffling around in the straw in the ark, testing out the boundaries of the fence line. Young animals of any breed are inherently endearing and these lively little creatures were no different as they barged about from one end of the enclosure to the other, halting occasionally to look at us, lifting their heads in the air and peering up at us as if to work out who these new humans were.

'There is a difference,' said Michael. 'That one is the smallest, the one by the gate is a bit bigger and the one who's just gone into the pig ark is the largest.'

'I'll leave you to think of some names then. Are you coming back?'

'No. I'll stay with them a bit longer.'

Given all I had read about pigs I had expected to have a deeper relationship with them than I did. As they got bigger they got pushier, particularly around feeding time, and you had to keep your wits about you or run the risk of getting knocked over. There was absolutely no malice in them but I still found them intimidating at times, particularly as they explored everything with their mouths, including the laces on shoes, buckles on wellie boots, toggles on coats – in short, if they could reach it, it was likely to end up in their mouths.

Michael felt much more at ease in their company, not least as we split our labour, me feeding the sheep whilst he fed the pigs, and so he spent more time with them. He named them Wee George, Middle George and Big George, a partial compromise given that they wouldn't be with us for very long.

We fed them on compound feed pellets, supplemented by vegetable peelings and acorns, which we would collect on our walks with the dogs. A few of our friends in the village liked to feed them their scraps as well but when we came to the autumn and a bountiful apple harvest we learned that pigs can have too much of a good thing.

'Wee George is sick.' Michael looked grim as he came back from the morning feed. 'He's not interested in food. Just lying there looking very sorry for himself.'

'Do you know what's wrong?'

'No. But I think he has to go to the vet.'

We looked at each other. Moving pigs wasn't as easy as moving sheep and we hadn't yet built the funnel we were going to use to load them up when we took them to the abattoir.

'Do you think he'll load up all right?'

'Probably, as he's feeling poorly. But the other two might barge in there with him if we're not careful.'

In fact, the other two pigs took one look at the trailer and disappeared to the far side of the enclosure. Wee George was so disinterested in life generally that he let us herd him gently in and then collapsed on the floor.

It didn't take the vet long to work out what the problem was.

'Have you been feeding him apples?'

'Yes. But not that many.'

'Could anyone else have been feeding him apples?'

'Our neighbours sometimes take food up so it's possible.'

'People think pigs can eat huge amounts of anything but you need to be careful with windfall. The fruit starts to ferment in their stomach. You can see his belly is extended and very uncomfortable. He's gorged himself so you might want to think about monitoring what the neighbours drop off as well as what you feed him.'

Thankfully all he needed was a few days' rest, and no more apples, but it was noticeable how that brief time of illness set him back. He never put on the weight the way his two brothers did. Wee George lived up to his name and stayed small.

Chapter 14

A step too far

❖ ❖ ❖

In 2008 Hugh Fearnley-Whittingstall and Jamie Oliver turned up on our TV screens, the former with a mini-series under the banner of *Hugh's Chicken Run* and the latter with a one-off programme called *Jamie's Fowl Dinners*. They had a shared mission of raising awareness of the appalling conditions of commercial poultry production. Faced with greater consumer knowledge, with people more aware about what they were buying, they hoped that the supermarkets could be lured away from cheap factory-farmed chicken and towards ethically reared, free-range birds.

They certainly caught the public's attention, but it was a controversial subject, with vested interests on all sides. Many consumers were so moved and horrified at what the programmes showed them that they did indeed change their buying habits and tried to purchase free-range chicken, not an easy thing to do as at the time free-range birds accounted for less than 5% of total production.[6] Others felt that the two chefs had no grasp on the reality of everyday life for the less privileged, where the family budget was already stretched to breaking point. Both poultry producers and the wider farming industry were up in arms, claiming that they were not the enemy but rather the victims of the supermarkets' stranglehold on pricing.

Both men were sticking their heads above the parapet, fully aware that they would get a strong reaction, positive and negative, as this was an emotive subject. We applauded their bravery, because there was no getting away from the brutal reality of how the chickens were treated. They were crammed into cages or barns, with no room to move or live a normal life, fed around the clock to bring them up to an acceptable weight as quickly as possible, and welfare issues came in a very poor second to making a profit on the operation, not an easy thing to do with the supermarkets paying unsustainable prices for the meat. The entire system was flawed, with blame to be laid at many doors, and no easy answers.

The situation was slowly changing for the better in the egg industry, with consumers more aware of the plight of battery-farmed chickens and willing to pay a premium for free-range eggs. Intensively reared meat birds had an equally miserable life,

---

[6] http://www.followthethings.com/chickenrun.shtml

and it made no sense to us to support one over the other. Our chickens provided us with all the eggs we needed, and when we wanted chicken for meat we bought it from our local butcher or a supermarket, choosing a free-range variety when we could. Even so, we wondered at times just how 'free-range' those chickens had been. The only way to know for sure what type of life that chicken had led would be to raise our own birds for meat and as we already ate our own pork and lamb, adding chickens seemed a natural extension.

We bought six eggs of a Sasso breed of chicken, which was supposed to be a good for meat, and put them under a couple of our permanently broody bantams. Five of them hatched and, once they were old enough, we sectioned off part of the chicken field so that we could monitor and control their feed. We would be feeding them bigger rations than our laying chickens and didn't want them to have to compete with our established flock for food. Commercial chickens are fed around the clock and as their ability to move is restricted in a crowded barn they expend very little energy, reaching the required weight quickly, within forty to fifty days. Our free-range birds would be foraging for their own food as well as the grain that we fed them and would sleep naturally at night, so we envisaged that they might need at least double that time to reach the right weight.

We took great pleasure in watching them grow from fluffy little bundles of golden fur to healthy, happy chickens but our pleasure was tempered by the knowledge that these birds had a limited life ahead of them and that we didn't have the option of taking them to an abattoir to do the killing for us. If you raise your own chickens for meat, then it is up to you to slaughter them. We had never killed an animal before and were dreading it, even though we felt we were doing it for all the right reasons.

'Who's going to do the evil deed?' Michael asked one evening. We had been talking about something else entirely but I knew what he meant as it had been niggling away at the back of my mind.

'It needs to be done quickly,' I said, skirting around the question. 'And cleanly. A good technique is essential.'

As usual, I had been reading up on the subject.

'I know that, but it's not exactly something that you can practise.'

The next day our friends Polly and Nick turned up on the doorstep with a dead pheasant. Nick used to be a butcher and they had far more experience than we did in preparing meat for cooking.

'This is for you.' They plonked it on the kitchen table.

'Thank you. We shall enjoy that.'

'No you won't. You're not eating it, we are. But we can talk you through how to snap a bird's neck and you can practise on our pheasant.'

This seemed an excellent idea. Before I knew it the bird had been thrust into my hands, instructions issued and everybody stood and looked at me expectantly. I took a deep breath and made what I thought would be the right twisting motion with my hands, but the neck remained intact.

'Do it as if you mean it,' said Nick. 'With conviction.'

I tried again but nothing happened.

'That doesn't look like conviction to me.'

The bird was taken out of my hands and passed over to Michael. With one deft movement he broke the neck and the question of who was going to do the evil deed had been answered.

A week later we decided it was time.

'How are we supposed to pick one?' I asked, as we stood in the field and watched our chickens pecking around happily in the grass.

'That one,' said Michael. 'It's the biggest.' He picked it up under one arm and carried it out of the field.

'Are you ok with this?' I asked.

'Yes and no. But if we're going to do it, let's get it over with.'

And with a quick twist it was done. The bird twitched violently for what was probably a few seconds, but felt much longer, and then lay limp in his hands.

Our next task was to pluck it, another new experience, and one best done quickly. Apparently the feathers would be harder to pull out the longer we left it. We hung it up in the garage so that we could get at it more easily and discovered two things. First was that there were far more feathers on a chicken than we had ever realised and second, that underneath all those feathers was a surprisingly scrawny bird.

'It seemed so fat and plump when it was in the field.' I untied the bird and weighed it in my hand. 'It's a good thing it's only us for dinner.'

'The next thing is to clean out the insides,' said Michael. 'And that's your job.'

I opened my mouth, ready to negotiate, but he forestalled me.

'I killed it. You can gut it.'

I nodded. It seemed only fair.

We all have different comfort levels about certain things. I could cope with maggots pouring out of a sheep with flystrike (more on that later) but I had an absolute horror of sticking my hand inside a dead chicken and pulling its innards out.

I cut off the head and then, bracing myself, pushed my hand inside the cavity and pulled out the guts and other organs.

'I think we can eat the heart and liver,' said Michael.

'You're on your own for that one,' I replied, taking the carcass to the sink and giving it a thorough rinse. As I did so, I thought about how a word, or an act, can change our perception of a creature. An hour ago this had been a bird, not just any bird but one of our birds, raised from a chick. Now it was a carcass.

The relationship and emotions involved with each of those words and concepts were quite different.

We had roast chicken for dinner the following night. It tasted delicious but the texture was different to shop-bought birds and required a bit more chewing. We used the leftovers the next day for a curry and everything else was boiled up to make a stock which went into a soup later in the week. It seemed important not to waste anything, to recognise that a creature had died so that we could eat, and to value it accordingly.

Over the next six weeks or so we killed and ate another three of our birds, which left just one. It would be cruel to leave it by itself so it joined the other chickens. The next time we chose to have chicken for a meal I bought it from the butcher. Michael didn't comment until we had finished eating it.

'We've still got one Sasso left.'

'I know. I don't want to kill it. It gets worse each time.'

Michael let out a long sigh. 'Me too.'

And so our last Sasso chicken was reprieved. I had mixed feelings about our foray into killing our own birds. On the one hand, I believed that if I was going to eat meat then I should take some responsibility for what happened to the animal or bird that died to feed me. Whether I killed it, or someone else did it, didn't change the fact that it died.

On a personal level, however, neither of us had the stomach for killing another living creature by our own hand. We had proved to ourselves that we could do it, and if Armageddon should arrive at some point in the future then we would be able to fall back on those survival skills, but we weren't comfortable with it. I'm sure that the few remaining groups of people who are totally self-sufficient in this modern age – the Inuits, the nomadic tribes of Mongolia, back-woodsmen in America and some of the older generations in rural Europe, for example – would be at a loss to understand this reluctance. However, whilst we were doing our best to live in a sustainable way, to provide a good life for our animals, we couldn't change the way we had been raised, couldn't ignore the cultural norms that shaped how we behaved and which influenced our attitudes towards life and death. Nothing in my life so far had prepared me for killing my own food. My parents didn't do it and I hadn't been bought up as a child to think it was normal. My hunter-gatherer instincts must have still been there but they were buried deep, smothered under the comfort blanket of having a supermarket always at hand. Our modern society has evolved to distance itself from death, pushing the responsibility onto other people. Whilst our ancestors had of necessity to be jacks-of-all-trades, we have specialists for every part of our lives. We go the garage to get our car fixed, the doctor for our health, the council to keep our roads in order and we rely on abattoirs and factory production lines to do our killing for us.

It's hardly surprising that we found it difficult. It was a step too far. We all have to walk our own road.

Chapter 15

A bad year

❖ ❖ ❖

After four years on our smallholding we were beginning to feel more confident of our abilities in managing this new way of life. I had acquired the habit of measuring each year by the cycles that defined it: from tupping to lambing, from the fresh spring pasture to haymaking, from the dark days of winter when the chickens laid few eggs to the long days of summer when we had more eggs than we knew what to do with. I gained a sense of comfort in recognising these patterns, of feeling grounded and having a purpose. My flock of sheep had grown in numbers as I had kept some of the ewe lambs for breeding and my relationship with them grew stronger each year as we got to know each other better.

There is a perception that sheep are boring, spending most of the day doing nothing more than eating, or sitting in the middle of a field chewing with the most vacant of expressions on their faces. I can see why this lack of activity might make them appear dull, but in fact they each had distinct personalities, and they were just doing what they were born to do and I found something calming in that. Whenever life got too hectic, my simple remedy was to sit with my sheep for half an hour. As I watched them doing nothing, a great advert for 'living in the now' if ever there was one, I would feel my frazzled brain slow down, and that brief respite would give me the ability to step back and gain some perspective.

When lambing time came around in this particular year I felt that I was on top of it. I thought I had been through the cycle enough times to recognise any potential difficulties and my mature ewes had consistently proven themselves to be wonderful mothers. Domino and Spot, two of the lambs that I had bred two seasons ago, were having their first lambing season so I would need to keep a closer eye on them, but I no longer suffered from the anxiety that had plagued me as I learnt the ropes in the earlier years.

Ellie was the first to produce with a pair of twins, one male, one female, both born prematurely. They were tiny and the girl lamb died later that day. Ellie had very little milk and so I had to supplement-feed the other one, who I called Little Man due to his diminutive size. I sat on a bale, the lamb in my lap sucking away at the bottle for all he was worth, and looked anxiously at Ellie.

Her pregnancy this year had really taken it out of her and I resolved that this would be her last lambing season. She could go into a well-deserved retirement.

Four days later Fatso produced triplets at three am in the morning. She had just finished as I arrived to feed Little Man and they all seemed fine. By seven am one of the lambs was looking very poor and Little Man had taken a turn for the worse. I carted them both back up to the house, put them in the dog cage in front of the Rayburn and hand-fed them every few hours. Before long they were bouncing around and could go back to the field. I breathed a sigh of relief and hoped that things would return to normal from now on.

A couple of mornings later I came down to find that Spot had produced triplets, between my two am visit and breakfast. As this was her first time I had hoped to be around to see the birth as the first hour is crucial, but both she and the lambs seemed in fine form. They had been licked clean, were steady on their feet, and were suckling. I carried out all my usual checks, found and removed the afterbirth and got on with my day. When I went down later that day one of the lambs was dead. As I went into the field I could see it was lying on the ground, Spot nudging it gently with her nose.

'Oh no. No, no.' I bent down and picked it up but it lay limp in my hands. There is something unbearably sad about losing an animal so newly born, so tiny and vulnerable, and it was made worse because I felt it was my fault. I must have missed something, although I had no idea what it could have been.

I looked anxiously at the remaining two lambs but they seemed fine. Two days later and they were both dead. I had rushed the last one to the vet who said it had picked up an infection and pumped it full of antibiotics but it was too far gone.

Several weeks later and Domino finally gave birth to twins. Four days after that we had yet again to rush one of them to the vet, but this time we caught it quickly and she survived.

'What did I do wrong?' I asked this question of my friend and sheep mentor Trish. I had phoned her, distraught, and she had come up to check on both me and Domino, who she was now giving a once-over to check that she was ok.

'Her teats are huge,' she said. 'Come and have a look. Her fleece is very thick; you'll have to pull it away to be able to see them.'

I could indeed see that the teats were engorged, at least twice the size that they should be.

'That happens sometimes,' she said. 'They're simply too big for the lamb to latch onto. They might have been that way from the time of birth or they might have swollen up further as the lambs struggled to draw off any milk. Another problem is that the duct at the end of the teat gets blocked by a plug of colostrum, like a lump of toffee, and so whilst it might look like the lamb is suckling, nothing is actually coming through. If that happens they can easily succumb to an infection.'

'So if I had noticed that in time, the lamb wouldn't have got sick?'

'Possibly. But it might have been something else altogether.' She looked at me sympathetically. 'I know it's hard but lambs die all the time, and they are at most risk in the early days. You've had a really good run going this many years without losing any.'

I knew this was true. I knew that there was an average mortality rate of 20% at lambing time. I knew that they were particularly vulnerable in those first few days when they relied solely on the colostrum from their mother's milk to give them immunity from infections. Even with that, they could still fall prey to hypothermia, dysentery, meningitis, scours and pneumonia. Statistics and facts are useful tools to help you guard against a range of possible outcomes. They don't offer a great deal of comfort when you've lost four lambs from such a small flock.

The part of my brain that loves an opportunity to make me feel guilty kicked into life. It whispered that I should have come down more often in the night. I was their shepherd and I was responsible. It was my job to keep them alive and healthy, and ignorance did not excuse failure on my part. This was indeed true but it was also true that I couldn't be watching my sheep twenty-four hours a day. The commercial farmer with five hundred to a thousand ewes to lamb would have someone there continually, the family taking shifts as the lambs came through thick and fast, both day and night, and even then they would lose some. We had just five ewes, and whilst we could, and did, organise our working lives around lambing, round-the-clock care simply wasn't a feasible option for us. Nor did I feel it was necessary. For the most part, although this year was proving to be an upsetting exception, our routine had worked well.

I could see that one of the reasons I was so upset was because these were my first deaths. It was a shock, and a difficult lesson to learn. Anyone who has livestock has no choice but to accept that death is part of life, that there will be bad years and good years. Even so, it took a while before I could stand and look at my flock and regain that sense of calm well-being that I had taken for granted before.

❖❖❖

We moved into early summer, a warm wet one, and a new problem emerged.

'Fancy popping down the pub for a drink?' asked Michael as I came back into the kitchen after my usual evening visit to the sheep.

'Not right now. I think Fatso has got flystrike.'

Michael grimaced.

There are all manner of ailments that sheep fall prey to, but flystrike is one of the worst. Damp, warm weather provides the ideal conditions for a blowfly, which can be either a bluebottle, a greenbottle or a blackbottle, to lay their eggs on the sheep. The fleece next to the skin provides an ideal breeding location, particularly if the fleece is soiled, but they will also lay eggs in an open wound or an infected area, even in the feet if the sheep is suffering from foot rot. A single fly can lay up to 250 eggs, which hatch as maggots within twelve hours, and they come into the world hungry. They attack and burrow into the flesh of their unwitting host, effectively eating the animal alive, and causing a slow, agonising death if not caught quickly. If they take too strong a hold, sometimes the only humane thing to do is to put the animal down.

'Are you sure that's the problem?'

'As sure as I can be. She's got a damp patch on her rump, she's kicking and twitching and running around as if she's trying to escape herself. And when she's not doing that she's just standing there, utterly miserable.' I went over to my medicine cupboard and pulled out two bottles I had not yet had cause to use but always kept in stock. Once flystrike has been diagnosed, immediate treatment is essential. One bottle was an eco-friendly treatment, relatively new to the market, and the other not at all eco-friendly, but with a proven history of being effective.

'Are you ready?' I raised an eyebrow at Michael.

'Do I need to come? I don't think I'd be very good with

maggots.'

'I need you to hold her. Best change into some old trousers. I'll see you down there.'

With Michael firmly holding Fatso at the front end, I donned some gloves and began to cut away at the patch of damp fleece on her rump. The closer to her skin I got, the more sodden it became. It smelt foul.

'Oh my lord.' I stepped back, holding my hand to my mouth.

'What is it?' asked Michael. 'Or would I rather not know?'

'It's maggots. So many maggots. Oh Fatso, you poor girl.'

I carried on cutting away at the damp fleece, Fatso's body juddering and twitching as I did so. The patch was much larger than it had appeared from the surface. Her skin was red and inflamed and covered in a writhing mass of maggots. It was somehow obscene.

'Right, I think I've cleared it all. I'm going to pour on the insecticide now so hold on tight. It might sting and we can't lose her.' I picked up the eco-friendly bottle.

'If she's that bad, shouldn't we just go with the normal stuff?'

Michael had buried his hands in Fatso's thick fleece and had braced himself as if he was prepared for her to start bucking like a bronco.

'I need to know if this works and the only way is to try it. If it doesn't we'll resort to the tried and tested poison.'

I unscrewed the cap and slowly poured a dribble of the insecticide onto a small area of skin as a test. Fatso lurched forwards but Michael held onto her and I stood open-mouthed in horrified fascination as the maggots reacted instantly, seeming almost to throw themselves off her in a desperate bid to escape the effect of the insecticide, twisting and jerking as if in agony, which I fervently hoped they were.

'It's working!' I applied some more, methodically working my way across the whole area of exposed flesh. The maggots continued to pour out, like rats from a sewer, but eventually the flow subsided and then died away altogether.

'Can I let her go now? My back is killing me.' Michael grimaced.

'Almost.' I picked up my clippers again. 'I just want to make absolutely sure that I haven't missed any.'

I clipped off another section of fleece from around the infected area, looking for more maggots, but the skin was its normal healthy pink.

'I think we're done. You can let her go.'

Fatso shot off, gave herself a huge shake from head to toe, and stood as far away from us as possible, still twitching.

Michael rubbed his back. 'After that we both deserve a pint.'

'You go. I'll stay for a while. There's been too much death in this family this year,' I said grimly. 'I am not losing any more sheep. I won't be too long.'

I raked up the clipped fleece and the dead maggots and put them in a bin bag for disposal later. Then I went and sat on my straw bale seat and watched Fatso. I was dimly aware of the gate opening beside me and Michael appeared, two bottles of beer in one hand and a packet of crisps in the other. Not for the first time was I grateful to have a pub within walking distance.

'You angel.' I took a long, grateful swig. He offered the crisps to me.

'Remember where my hands have been.'

'You had gloves on.'

'I know. Even so, until I've washed, no nibbling for me.'

'I'll feed you then. Open wide.' He popped a crisp in my mouth. 'Good practice for when you're old and senile and can't find your mouth.'

'I'll look forward to that.'

We sat there in quiet companionship, our eyes following Fatso as she tentatively began to nibble at the grass.

'It's amazing how quickly they bounce back,' observed Michael.

I nodded. 'They're far more resilient than we are. I'd be a basket case if I'd had those maggots inside me.'

'It helps that they don't have too much going on between their ears.' Michael picked up the bottles. 'I'm going to put some dinner on. If you're not back in twenty minutes I'll feed it to the dogs.' He looked at me pointedly.

'I'll be back. I promise.'

I got up and walked slowly around the flock, checking that no-one else had any damp patches or was acting strangely. I would have to keep an eye on Fatso over the next few days, not just for another outbreak of maggots but also to check that the bare patch of skin didn't get infected. For the moment, as far as I could tell, everyone looked healthy. I walked back down the lane to the house with a warm sense of satisfaction inside me. Nobody was going to die today.

❖❖❖

Autumn had arrived, the capricious, languid warmth of summer dancing off into the distance, soon to become no more than a memory. The air had a crisp, cool feel to it and the hills around us were turning red-gold as the bracken died back.

Chickens are drama queens. Not a day goes by without some minor catastrophe that requires a lot of squawking and flapping about. However as I stood by the kitchen sink one bright autumn morning it seemed to me that they were making more noise than usual. I walked through the garden and over to the gate to see if anything was wrong.

The fox was on the far side of the enclosure. Whilst so many of these predators were thin and mangy, this looked like a young dog- fox in his prime, his pelt gleaming richly in the sunshine. I could see golden feathers in the grass at his feet, and a bird-shaped body hunched in an unnatural position. He lifted his head and met my gaze, black eyes bright and unreadable. The second before my instincts kicked in and I reached for the gate, shouting and flapping my arms, he turned and was gone, disappearing into the bracken on the edge of the enclosure. I had the distinct impression that he'd known what I was going to do before I did.

The chickens were beside themselves. I walked over to the mound of feathers and found it to be the last of the Sasso birds, the one we had decided not to eat ourselves. Her reprieve from death had been short-lived. I must have startled him before he had a chance to really get going because she was still largely intact and I couldn't see any other bodies. I went back to the chickens, and did a headcount. All present and correct – bar one.

Tilly was missing. She had been one of a pair, the first birds we had bought. She was a Welsummer and had a tendency to wander, often flying out of the enclosure and into the field, unlike most of the flock who stayed in safer confines. I had a feeling that the urge to search for greener pastures had cost her dearly. Foxes were canny creatures and would regard birds that strayed away from the flock as easy prey. I went out into the field, scanning the hillside for any signs of a body, but there was nothing to be seen. I began to search more methodically, my eyes down to the ground, walking back and forth, and eventually I found a few feathers, from their colouring unmistakably hers.

There was nothing else left of her.

It may have been that the fox had taken her back to his den and then come back for more. Foxes tended to hunt at night, but young animals, newly independent and having to fend for themselves, were known to hunt in daylight. There was every chance the fox would be back.

I returned to the enclosure and went round our fencing on my hands and knees, trying to find out how he had got in. Pulling the bracken away in the far corner, I found a place where the earth had been dug away and the fence shredded, leaving a gap barely big enough for me to fit four fingers beneath. It didn't seem large enough for a fox to get under, but I had seen the way cats could flatten themselves to get through tiny gaps and there was no reason to think a fox would be any less adept at getting into places it wasn't wanted.

We repaired and reinforced the fence and made a point of running the dogs around the outside of the enclosure to see if their scent might deter the fox from coming back. We also increased the number of visits we made during the day.

Further down the valley, some farmers and other smallholders had their flocks completely wiped out by foxes, twenty birds or more at a time butchered in a killing frenzy. The next weekend the farmers brought their hunting terriers out and set them loose in the woods along the valley. We didn't have any more visits from the fox after that.

I had mixed feelings about this. Until I kept chickens, I had no problems with foxes and enjoyed catching a fleeting glimpse of them out on the hills. I knew they needed to eat like any other animal and were only doing what came naturally. Some of our friends accepted the loss of an occasional chicken as the natural way of things. I might have grudgingly come round to that way of thinking myself, if not for the fact that they rarely seemed to take enough just to eat. The dilemma was caused by what seemed to my human eyes to be a random killing spree. I was probably anthropomorphising their actions but it felt like it was an act of mindless cruelty, and inherently wasteful of life.

To put the case for the fox, it has been argued that it is in part the panic and noise of the birds being attacked, particularly in the enclosed space of the henhouse, that cause the fox to overreact, to be overtaken by blood lust. Also there is the argument that foxes can only carry one bird in their mouths at a time. They will come back to collect the other corpses if they are not disturbed and so sometimes it is not quite as wasteful as it seems.

Predictably our human response to any animal threatening or killing our food supply is to deliver instant and fatal retribution. The fox gets the same treatment as the bear and the wolf before it, but perhaps we are guilty of having double standards. We consider the fox to be the villain of the piece because we think it kills indiscriminately and wastefully. Yet we farm our animals on an industrial scale, often in shameful and cruel conditions, and then throw away about a third of the food we buy every year. And whilst that wasted food, be it chicken, pork or beef, may come wrapped in cellophane so that we have no connection to the animal it once was, the blunt truth is that it ended up in our rubbish bin for no other reason than it had passed its sell-by date or our plates were so full that we couldn't eat everything on it. It would appear that we can break our own rules about eating sustainably and not to excess, but other living creatures must abide by them or pay a heavy price.

❖❖❖

New Year's Eve arrived and, as was my habit at this time of year, I reserved a few hours of the day to read back over my diaries and remind myself of what sort of year we had lived through. It had not been the best of years. I hadn't entered into this life with rose-tinted glasses. I knew that it would be hard graft, that things wouldn't always go to plan, but I had always held the belief, naively in retrospect, that it would mainly be a positive experience, full of the promise of new life, of growth, of being at one with the natural world.

I still had faith in that belief, still loved the life we lived but, reading back through my thoughts and emotions, I could see that I'd had no perception that death would play such a large part in it, or how ruthless and cruel the natural world could be, a far cry from the gentle and benign entity that I had liked to think it was.

Neither had I understood that there were so many ways for an animal to die. Obviously there was our conscious decision, one not taken lightly, to raise our livestock knowing that we would kill them for meat, but once nature took a hand outcomes became random, sudden and unpredictable. A fox could take a chicken right under your nose, flystrike could overwhelm a ewe within twenty-four hours, a lamb could live or die on a whim, and then there was my own inexperience and ignorance to add to the melting pot. It was becoming ever clearer to me that the line between life and death was a thin one and that the notion of security, or being able to protect oneself and one's animals from that grim reality, was not something to be relied upon.

Some lessons in life hurt, the knowledge and experience they give hard-won. At times the price paid can feel as if it was too high but perhaps, in a perverse sense, these are the best lessons. You can't learn everything by reading a book, by going on courses, or by talking to people who know more than you do. Some things you just have to do for yourself and if you make mistakes along the way, that is all part of the learning process. What matters is to make sure you don't repeat them and that you can move on without being crippled by guilt or a lack of confidence.

I could see that this testing year had changed me, giving me a greater understanding of how life and death were a team and that you can't have one without the other, and also providing an awareness of my own fallibility. I felt stronger because of it. Hopefully it would make me a better custodian of all my animals but this new awareness went beyond that. I had seen the consequences of being predator or prey, of being born strong or weak, and of being ignorant or experienced. The stark principle of the survival of the fittest meant much more to me now than just a set of words because I had seen how the natural world didn't stop to consider whether an animal deserved to live or die. A set of circumstances would run their course, each interaction building up to another, until the conclusion was often inevitable.

I also had the disturbing sense that we humans had reached a stage in our development where we considered ourselves to be above it all. We thought we were the masters, in complete control of our world. There was no problem we couldn't solve, no situation we couldn't bend to our will. This seemed a misguided assumption and one that might end badly for us. Our chicken Tilly paid a high price for being on the wrong side of the fence, for thinking she was safe, and on the days when the excesses of the human race weighed heavily on my mind, I couldn't help but think that one day we might pay a similar price. When it comes down to the survival of the fittest, the natural world holds the winning hand.

'Are you still reading those diaries of yours?' Michael

appeared in the bedroom door. 'It's New Year's Eve! Time to get ready. We've got a party to go to.'

I snapped the diaries shut. He was quite right. It was time to welcome in the new year with good friends. Time to appreciate the lessons of the old year and move on to a new one. Hopefully, balance would be restored and this coming year would be a better one.

And, thankfully, it was.

Chapter 16

Understanding donkeys

❖ ❖ ❖

'That donkey of yours is pregnant,' said Liz, our local representative from the Donkey Sanctuary.

'She can't be. She's not been anywhere near a stallion.' I peered at Bella closely. It was true she did look a little rounder than when she had first come to us, but I'd assumed that was because she'd had too much grass, and donkeys get overweight very quickly.

'How long have you had her?'

I thought back. 'Maybe a year.'

'The gestation period is between eleven to fourteen and a half months.' She nodded to herself. 'So she was pregnant when she came to you.'

'Wow. This is going to take a bit of getting used to.' I worked out the maths. 'So we've got a month or two to prepare.'

'I shouldn't think so. More like a week or two if you're lucky. Maybe less.' She walked round to Bella's rear end and bent down. 'See how swollen the udder is. It'll go up and down a bit for the last four weeks of pregnancy. The milk will start to run in the last seventy-two hours. Then you'll know the birth is imminent.'

I felt the old, familiar feeling of being in a place where I had no experience yet again. Something of this must have shown on my face as Liz gave me a reassuring smile.

'You'll be fine. They usually give birth at night and prefer to be alone. It shouldn't take more than forty minutes and she'll probably do it all herself. Donkeys are tough little creatures.'

'Is there anything I need to do?'

'Just keep an eye on her. If you do have any complications it's a job for the vet.'

I had grown very fond of Bella. She was an affectionate animal, and would always come up to me for a scratch and a cuddle each time I visited her. We had taken her out occasionally for a walk with Snari on a lead rope, just to break the monotony of being in one place every day, but it was a slow and painful process, with much standing still on her part and a lot of unproductive pulling on ours. I knew that in the past donkeys had played an essential role in rural and isolated communities, transporting water, wood and other essential supplies, as well as cultivating the land and transporting goods to market. If we had been relying on Bella to move anything anywhere we'd have starved before it arrived. I decided that I must be doing something wrong. There had to be a knack to dealing with donkeys and so, after a particularly unsuccessful attempt at taking her for a walk, I enrolled myself on a handling day run by the sanctuary to find out what it was.

The day began with a brief overview of where donkeys came from and an explanation of how important they had been historically, and still were, in certain parts of the world. Descended from African wild asses, they've had a close relationship with the human race for centuries, and have long been used as a beast of burden.

'Most people think donkeys are similar to horses, but they're very different.' The lady running the training day was understandably a donkey fan. 'Much more intelligent. Much more interesting. Horses are flight animals. If they feel in danger their immediate reaction is to run. It's an instinctive response with little consideration behind it. The donkey prefers to think about it, to evaluate the threat and then decide on a course of action. They have a very strong sense of self-preservation, and if they think something isn't in their own best interests they won't be bullied or coerced into doing it. This character trait has gained them the reputation of being stubborn and difficult to handle.'

There was much nodding of heads around me. Obviously I wasn't the only one having trouble motivating their animal.

'They also have different physical attributes compared to the horse. Most noticeably are those huge ears, which help keep them cool but also provide them with an acute sense of hearing. Unlike horses, donkey's coats are not waterproof and this is why we always recommend that you provide your donkey with a shelter if keeping them outside. And lastly, they make a very different noise to the horse, a distinctive "hee-haw" braying sound. The "hee" comes on an in-breath, the "haw" on an out-breath. Nothing sounds quite like a donkey.'

We broke up for lunch, giving us all a chance to swap stories about our stubborn beasts, and then came the bit I was looking forward to, the correct way to handle a donkey so that it did what you wanted it to do.

'We'll begin with the basics.' Our instructor ran a critical eye around the group. 'How many of you have trouble keeping your donkeys moving on a lead rein?'

Every single head nodded.

'The important thing is never to pull a donkey. The minute you pull in one direction, they'll resist and pull in the opposite direction.' She walked off with a donkey on a loose lead rein. It followed her with a docile obedience that seemed completely at odds with my personal experience.

'See where I'm standing? Right by its shoulder. Not out in front of it. Not pulling on the rope. There's no point in getting into a pulling competition. They're very strong, much stronger than a horse of a similar size.'

After a bit more instruction it was time for us to split into pairs, each pair with one of the rescue donkeys, and practise the art of walking shoulder by shoulder.

'Do you want to go first?' asked my partner, Carol, who had very recently taken on a rescue donkey.

'Not really. But best get it over with I guess.' I stood by the donkey's shoulder and walked on. It didn't budge. I walked on another step and still it didn't move.

'Now what?' I looked at Carol for help. 'If I walk on, I'll end up pulling it.'

'Remember, no pulling. Be definite, be patient, but no pulling.' The instructor had one of those voices that carried a long way. I looked around, guilt all over my face, but she was standing on the other side of the field, talking to another couple. I handed the reins to Carol. 'Why don't you have a go?'

Carol fared no better than I. By this time the instructor had worked her way over to us. She didn't seem surprised that we hadn't moved more than a few paces.

'It takes time. These donkeys don't know you so don't worry too much if they aren't too enthusiastic. I'm sure you'll do better with your own animal.'

I remembered those words as I led Bella out of the field she shared with Snari and down to the small paddock where we could more easily keep an eye on her in these last days of her pregnancy. I had been trying to walk shoulder to shoulder for weeks now and had come to the conclusion that some things just weren't meant to be. I was resigned to the fact that we'd get to where we wanted to go at a pace that suited Bella, and from the smug look on her face, she obviously felt that was the way it should be.

A few days after I moved her into her new field her milk started to run. A day later I popped down in the late evening to check on her and found her in the far corner of the field, lying down and straining.

I crouched down by the fence and waited to see what happened next. The last thing I wanted to do was to frighten her or put her off, but she knew I was there and seemed unconcerned. Half an hour went by with no sign of her foal coming out despite her efforts and I began to get worried, but then a nose and two front feet appeared. Shortly afterwards she gave a great heave and the foal slid out.

After that it was a textbook birth. I made myself more comfortable and watched, entranced, as she licked her newborn son clean. I saw him take his first wobbly steps, shared her concern as his legs collapsed beneath him and he fell, and breathed a sigh of relief as he got up again. I saw the tenderness in the way she nudged him onto the teat, and the protective way she followed his progress as he grew more confident on his feet. And then she looked at me. Years later I still struggle to find the words to express what passed between us, but it felt as if it was a recognition that we had shared a moment of intimacy, that I had been witness to an event that few humans have the privilege of seeing.

'He's beautiful, Bella,' I said quietly. 'You're doing a great job.'

She nodded her head at me, as if in agreement, and I laughed.

By this stage in our smallholding life I had seen many newly-born creatures and it was always special, always felt like a miracle, but I realised that there was something different about this particular birth. This young foal wasn't here for my benefit. I wouldn't eat him, or raise him to breed other animals that I would eat in the future. Instead I could just enjoy him for what he was. It made a difference somehow and it was something that I would ponder on over the coming months.

We called him River and he grew quickly, turning into a boisterous, pushy youngster. As the months passed the testosterone kicked in and he became a real handful, constantly trying to mount Bella, who gave him both barrels on a regular basis which deterred him not at all. He was also testing the boundaries with us, playful nips becoming not quite so playful. I sought advice from the Donkey Sanctuary and they said this was a common problem. Previously placid and friendly young donkey stallions can become aggressive both to other donkeys and to humans once their hormones start to take effect and will try to mate with a female, be it their mother or sisters or any other donkey, once they are a year old. This can lead to unwanted foals or birth defects. Geldings are usually more predictable and easier to handle, but it depends on when they were castrated. If a two-year-old has learned its own strength and become aggressive then even after being castrated, those learned behaviour patterns may remain. The sanctuary recommended that a colt should be castrated as young as possible, from six months onwards, not just to solve behavioural problems but also because the process was less traumatic in a young animal and they recovered more quickly. The bottom line was that stallion donkeys do not make good pets, a fact the sanctuary knew better than most as those stallions often ended up at their door, in need of a home because their owners had bought a sweet little foal as a pet for their children and ended up with something far from sweet.

The subject of castration is not an easy one, and on the one hand I didn't like to do it, but I understood the thinking that it is better for the donkey to experience the minor discomfort of the operation than to spend its life in an unsuitable environment, perhaps isolated or mistreated due to being difficult to handle, or frustrated and stressed at being permanently kept apart from female donkeys.

Even after castration we were advised that River should be kept apart from Bella for two months. This would have been difficult to arrange, but then we had a stroke of luck in that an old friend of mine who had a smallholding on the other side of Abergavenny offered to take him. She had always wanted a donkey and needed a companion for her horse, a gelding. We breathed a sigh of relief. River went off to a new home and Bella was left in peace with Snari once more. I visited him on numerous occasions after his operation and, whilst he was still boisterous and very nosy about what was going on around him, the aggression had gone. It had been the right thing to do.

Chapter 17

From pig to pork

❖ ❖ ❖

Some of the lanes in the hills that surrounded us were barely single track. They wiggled their way over and around the contours, one blind bend after another. By the early summer the hedgerows had filled out, spiky hawthorn and rampant brambles poking into the road with malicious intent, running scratchy fingers along the faded paintwork on the side of the Land Rover as we drove along a particularly narrow lane faster than we should have. We were late for a meeting but there was never much traffic, just as well because passing places were few and far between.

'Are you sure this is the right way?' I asked.

'You're the one with the map,' said Michael.

'I know, but they said to go along here for a couple of miles and it feels like longer than that by now.'

'It's just a slow road.' Suddenly he slammed on the brakes and we screeched to a halt.

I looked up with a jolt from the map to find we were inches away from the front of a shiny red tractor with a sheep trailer on the back.

'Looks like we're reversing. Keep your eyes peeled for a track or a passing place.'

I kept my eyes dutifully peeled but nothing materialised. We had to reverse all the way back to the T-junction. The tractor driver wound his window down as he came level with us.

'There's another trailer coming behind me. Shouldn't be more than a few minutes.' He gave a cheery wave and chugged off.

'Great,' I muttered crossly. 'Now we're really going to be late.'

We were on our way to a farm to watch the process of butchering a pig carcass. We wondered if this was a job that we could do ourselves at some point in the future and wanted to see how it was done professionally first. The enterprising young couple who lived at this farm took their animals to the local abattoir for slaughter in the normal way, but had invested in a purpose-built cold room at their farm where they could butcher the carcasses themselves. It saved them money on their own livestock and, as the word had spread, many of the local smallholders had chosen to use them. It wasn't a huge money earner for them but it provided another income stream to support the farm.

Ten minutes later the second trailer had passed through and we could resume our journey. Eventually we pulled off the lane and up a track to the farm. To our left was an open-sided barn neatly stacked with hay, in front of us was a whitewashed stone cottage with a child's cycle lying on its side on a handkerchief-sized lawn, and to our right was a squat, single-storey building with no windows. We parked up alongside the barn, the slamming of our car doors setting off a couple of sheepdogs chained up somewhere out of sight. A large metal door slid open in the building to our right and a man wearing a white apron called out a welcome.

We introduced ourselves, made our apologies for being late, and then took stock of our surroundings as the husband and wife team, Mark and Carol, gave us a tour. Everything inside the building was white, the walls, ceiling, cupboards, the tiled floor, lit by two strips of glaringly bright fluorescent lighting that were already hurting my eyes. In the centre were two stainless steel cutting tables, empty apart from an intimidating collection of axes, cleavers, saws, choppers and knives. A bright red portable radio provided the only splash of colour, perched cheerily on a shelf next to a pile of paperwork. It seemed a sterile, silent, cold place, as you might expect given its function, and markedly different to the world immediately outside. Farms are vibrant places, full of life, noise and movement. As I stood next to the cutting table, shivering slightly due to the fridge-like temperature, the contrast was stark.

Behind this main room was the cold storage area, a huge walk-in refrigerator where three pig carcasses were hung on hooks, ready to be processed. I swallowed as I looked at them. A few days ago these had been our pigs, Wee George, Middle George and Big George. Where once had been three distinct personalities, now there was just flesh and bone.

'We thought we'd do the smallest one this afternoon,' said Mark. 'We may not get it finished, but it will be enough to give you an idea where all the different bits of meat come from.'

I nodded, surprised that it would take so long. It was a relatively quick job to butcher a lamb carcass if you knew what you were doing and I had assumed it would only take a little longer for a pig. As the minutes turned into hours we saw first-hand just how much more meat a pig produced, a mind-boggling quantity of hams, tenderloins, ribs, belly pork, roasting joints, chops and hocks, sausages and bacon. Mark explained what they were doing as they went along and I was impressed at their knowledge, at the deft way they handled knives and choppers, lethally sharp and which could have so easily sliced off a finger with a moment's inattention.

'Do you want middle, back or streaky bacon,' asked Carol,

'or a mixture of all of them?'

Michael and I looked at each other blankly.

'Back bacon comes from the loin area, along the backbone,' she explained. 'Streaky comes from the belly and has more fat which makes it more flavoursome and middle is back and streaky in one cut.'

We decided we'd go for a mixture of streaky and back bacon.

'We're going to need another freezer,' I muttered to Michael as I saw the length of meat that was being put aside for bacon and tried to imagine how many slices that would provide.

'Wait until you see how many sausages you get,' said Mark. 'You're not keeping all three carcasses for your own consumption, are you?'

'No, we're giving half a pig away as payment for use of the land and we'll sell off maybe another one and a half to cover the costs of buying and raising them. That leaves one pig for us, which should be plenty.'

He nodded. 'Even if you're big meat eaters it should see you through a year.'

After two hours most of Wee George had disappeared from the cutting table and had been stored in the cold room. As we grew progressively colder, the chill working its way deep into our bones while we stood and watched, our hosts grew warmer, peeling off layers beneath their white coats. It was a physically demanding job.

'Our pigs aren't particularly big ones,' I remarked, as they stopped for a drink of water. 'What do you do if someone brings in a Large White?'

Large Whites are big pigs, a third again as big as ours, with long, wide-backed bodies that make them an ideal choice for hams and bacon. They produce so much meat that they have had the misfortune to become one of the primary breeds used in commercial meat production. I sized up the length of the cutting table and wondered if a Large White would even fit on it.

'Most of our customers are smallholders and they prefer smaller pigs,' said Carol. 'I'm not sure what we'd say if someone rang up wanting a pig that size done.'

'I know exactly what I'd say,' grunted Mark.

'Which is why I don't let you pick up the phone,' came the wry rejoinder.

Mark put down his knives and stretched his back. 'I think we're done for today. The sausages are a big job in their own right so we'll leave that for tomorrow.'

We thanked them both profusely for allowing us to come and see how it was all done, agreed we would come back in a couple of days once all three pigs were finished and climbed back into the Land Rover. I turned up the fan heater, a pointless exercise as I knew it would scarcely have warmed up by the time we reached home, and rubbed my fingers to try and get some warmth back into them.

'I feel completely exhausted and I didn't do anything except watch them,' I said. 'There's no way we could ever do that ourselves. We don't have the space and all the equipment would cost a fortune.'

'Some things are best left to the professionals,' said Michael. 'We can't do everything.'

I thought back to the times when families raised a pig in a yard at the rear of their house, feeding it on the slops and leftovers. They would hang it up and slaughter it themselves, the whole family involved in the process which could easily take two to three days, and nothing would be wasted. The blood was made into blood pudding or sausages, the intestines were cut into short pieces and fried, the head and any leftovers were boiled up to make brawn pate and the bowels were sometimes cleaned and used as a casing for the sausages.

Going back no further than two or three generations, young children would have been brought up to think that this was a perfectly normal thing to do. How quickly things change. We all live according to the time we are born into, developing the skills necessary to survive in our particular environment. Today our essential life skills seem to centre around being able to use a smartphone and a computer and to distance ourselves as much as possible from anything so messy as butchering our own meat. I tried to imagine holding a knife in my hand and slitting the throat of one of the pigs myself. If my only other option was to starve, then I knew I would somehow find the strength of mind to do it, but it would be deeply distressing, and whilst I lived in a world where I could pay an abattoir to do it, quickly and humanely, then that was a choice I would continue to make. The butchering of a carcass was something different, as by that stage it had become meat, and no longer an animal. The connection from one living being to another had been severed.

I wondered what the families of times past would think if they could see into the future, with people picking up a couple of pork chops wrapped in polystyrene and cling film from a chiller cabinet in a supermarket, or even ordering it online and having it delivered to the door. Would they envy us, or pity us?

Chapter 18

Orphan

❖ ❖ ❖

Orphan lambs are an inevitable part of the lambing cycle. Their mothers may die during the lambing process or reject them for various reasons immediately after birthing them. First-time mothers in particular can be so confused and distressed at the whole process that they will literally walk away from a lamb, or lose patience if it takes too long to find the teat. Some sheep won't have enough milk for triplets, or may even produce quads, a rare occurrence but not unknown. Raising orphan lambs is a time-consuming business and so where possible the farmer will try to pass the lamb on, introducing it to a ewe with only one lamb who has milk to spare.

However there are times when there is no alternative but to bottle-feed the lamb, feeding them every two to three hours for the first two weeks, and then every four hours for the next few weeks. It is a full-time commitment, one that is often taken on by the farmer's wife with the help of the children, but given that the whole family will be working together over the lambing season, it adds an extra burden that many farmers don't really want. Orphan lambs often never get over those first few difficult hours of their lives and can struggle to gain the weight needed to get a good price for them at market. Every penny counts on a farm.

In all our time of keeping sheep we never lost a ewe whilst lambing and never needed to completely hand-rear a lamb. We had a few occasions where we supplement-fed a lamb because the ewe had a poor supply of milk but it was nothing as onerous as the round-the-clock care that a real orphan needed. We were very lucky in that our Jacobs were calm, efficient mothers and could usually cope with triplets.

But then one day I came down to the woodpile by our back gate and found a lamb out on the lane. I guessed she was at least four weeks old, stocky and strong, and she looked at me with a bright, bold curiosity. I walked slowly up to our gates, just in case I might frighten her, and looked up and down the lane to see if one of the local farmers was moving their flock around. The lane was empty. She was on her own. I looked down to find she had stuck her nose through the gate and was trying to suck on my trouser leg.

I couldn't leave her out there. The lane bent sharp right and then straight down to the main road, no place for a lone youngster. I opened the gate and she shot past me, up the steps and into the garden where she promptly proceeded to have an exploratory nibble at the rose bushes before deciding that our lawn was a more satisfying option. She followed me quite happily into the chicken field, although the chickens didn't think much of the arrangement, clucking indignantly as she stuck her nose inside the door to the henhouse and then began chasing them round the field. I left her there while I phoned around to try and find where she might have come from, hoping the henhouse would still be in one piece when I returned.

It didn't take too long to find her owner, a farmer we knew well, just at the end of our lane.

'She's a nightmare that one,' he sighed. 'Her mother died giving birth so I've bottle-fed her but she's always getting out. She's more trouble than she's worth. She's yours if you want her.' There was a hopeful pause at the other end of the phone. 'She'd fit in well with your little flock.'

I considered it for a moment. I really didn't want an orphan lamb. We'd just finished lambing and life was returning to normal.

'She only needs feeding twice a day now,' he added helpfully.

And so Mitsie came to join us. She was a character with a capital 'C' but as time went on I began to wonder if she knew she was a sheep. She would run to us as soon as she heard our voices, almost as keen on the close physical contact as she was on the milk we brought with us. She would push her little body hard against my legs, stick her nose up in the air and shut her eyes with the closest thing a sheep can manage to a blissful expression while I scratched under her chin and round her ears. The chickens were her second family, to the point that I would occasionally find her sleeping inside the henhouse. Given the size of the door, this was no mean feat, and eventually became one of the reasons we decided it was time to move her in with our sheep, before she wrecked the thing completely.

A flock is a close-knit unit and whilst my Jacobs tolerated Mitsie, she was always an outsider, grazing slightly apart from them, resting away from them. She had no mother to run to when threatened, no-one to teach her how to behave, or to gather her up and keep her safe when the flock was moving. She would see the other lambs suckling and try to copy them, but the ewes knocked her firmly out of the way. She wasn't welcome. It didn't help that she looked completely different, so very white compared to their coloured fleeces, so obviously not of the same breed. I discussed it with my fellow smallholders and many of them had seen this isolation with the bottle-fed lambs, even if the sheep were the same breed.

I hoped that in time the barriers might come down but they never did. She still ran to me when I came into the field, even after she no longer needed to be hand-fed. It was a lesson in what happens when you upset the natural balance. If the farmer hadn't intervened and fed her in those early weeks, she would not have survived, so it was a choice that we were happy to live with, although far from ideal. My fervent hope was that when she had her own lambs in the future she would finally get a sense of belonging but she confounded my hopes here by steadfastly refusing to let any ram anywhere near her. This didn't stop her trying to steal lambs from the other ewes, hardly an action that was going to foster any chance of acceptance within the flock. She was here to stay though, so they would just have to get along as best they could. As for me, all she had to do was run up to me and thump her bullet head against my thigh, demanding a scratch under the chin, and I somehow forgot how maddening she was.

Chapter 19

Ain't got no roots

❖ ❖ ❖

I've never been very good at staying in one place or sticking to one thing. Since I graduated with a degree in Business Studies over thirty years ago I have changed jobs seventeen times and lived in fourteen different houses. Some jobs lasted a few years, some no more than a few months. I have the attention span of a gnat, very little patience, and am addicted to change, to pastures new. Commitment is a scary word.

These are terrible qualities for a person who is trying to live off the land. It takes years to build up a flock, or for a tree to produce fruit in sufficient quantities to make it worthwhile harvesting. It takes patience to learn all the skills required to be a competent smallholder. And it takes commitment to stick with it through the bad times as well as the good ones, rather than moving on when the going gets tough. It's a long game.

It's just as well that I didn't have to go through an interview process to begin this new career in animal husbandry and food production because no-one in their right mind would have hired me. However, I can put forward one argument in my defence. This wasn't a job. It was never about money, power or ambition. It was, to coin a much overused phrase, a lifestyle choice.

Jumping into a new lifestyle inevitably leads to challenges: taking a leap into the unknown, learning new skills, deciding where you stand on the moral and ethical issues that come with that new life, being open to change and ready to deal with uncertainty. A lifestyle change is all about embracing life, and on that basis perhaps I wasn't quite such a useless candidate after all. Regularly changing jobs meant that I had gained the skill of picking things up quickly, of recognising what needed to be learnt as a priority. I was used to the sense of trepidation that comes when you are doing things for the first time and enjoyed the challenge of testing myself in new ways. That past experience helped me to adapt to our new lifestyle although my lack of patience remained a black mark in the box. When you organise your life around nature and animals you need to accept that they will have the last word, but it took a long time for this to sink in.

Even though I felt that my background would help me through this new life, it soon became obvious that I would have to change and grow as a person if I was going to last the course.

With each new challenge overcome, each new skill slowly and painstakingly acquired, I felt those changes were beginning to take place, but the one thing that eluded me was a sense of putting down roots.

Each year the summer came round and with it a sense of being able to relax. Much of the hard work of the year had been done and now we could enjoy the results: watching the lambs racing along the length of the field each night as the sun went down, casting a critical eye over our fruit and vegetables to see if they might be potential prize winners in the village show. It was a period of respite, a time to slow down and make the most of the long summer days.

Of course there were still jobs to be done. This year we had kept the sheep off one of the fields so that we could grow it for hay. Previously we had bought hay in, but the combination of high prices during the previous winter and the fact that our flock was getting bigger gave us a good reason to grow our own.

We would need help with the harvesting. The majority of smallholders along our valley, ourselves included, owned or rented small parcels of land and worked on limited budgets. Investing thousands of pounds in the equipment needed to make hay was neither sensible given the small scale of their holding, nor financially viable given the cost, and so instead they had arrangements with the larger farms to cut and bale their hay for them. Our farmer neighbour Colin was happy to add us to his list of fields to be cut that summer and so all we had to do was to watch it grow and hope for a good spell of settled weather when the time came to cut it.

There is both an art and a wealth of science behind the process of turning grass into hay. Our knowledge could be summed up in six words from the well-known proverb, 'make hay while the sun shines', but there was more to it than that. According to the *Irish Farmers Journal* hay should be cut at the end of a sunny day when the seed heads are not quite ripe and the leaf is at its maximum. Moisture content should have dropped to 70% at the time of cutting and should drop further down to 20% after it has dried out. Soluble sugars should be around 29%, crude protein at 10–12% and the DMD (Dry Matter Digestibility for those of us who might not be familiar with the term) should be between 65–70%.

The British Grassland Society has three words of advice on the potential pitfalls of making hay: 'Weather, weather, weather'. Weather is probably the most important factor in making good hay, and the most unpredictable. Baling hay when it is too wet means you could end up with mouldy, unuseable fodder, but at the other end of the scale if the hay is too dry it loses its nutrient value.

We didn't have to concern ourselves with any of the above. Colin had all his own land to cut and bale, then he had his list of long-standing customers and friends to attend to – and then he had us. As newcomers we were understandably at the bottom of the pile. It would get done when it got done.

There are four steps to the process. It begins with the cutting, best done around mid-June typically, and in the afternoon if we lived in a world where the weather allowed us to operate by the textbook. After cutting comes 'tedding' where the grass is lifted and fluffed up so the entire crop can dry out, not just the layer that is at the top. We had our own term for this, 'whirling and twirling', as that seemed to describe more aptly what the machinery did. Thirdly, the hay is raked into lines or 'windrows' which make it easier to bale it up without wasting anything and then, finally, it is baled. The larger farms, particularly those with cattle, prefer the big round bales but for the smallholder, who will probably have to stack and store the bales by hand, the old-fashioned small square bales are preferred. The whole process takes three to four days and requires sunny, dry weather for the duration.

In the old days making hay would have been a communal affair, with friends and families roped in and neighbours working together to get the hay baled and stacked. Now it's all done by machine, one man in his tractor and trailer. Like so much of farming today it has become a solitary affair.

From early June we watched Colin as he and his tractor worked their way round the valley, his progress easy to track as the fields turned from knee-high grass to short, prickly stubble.

If it had been a wet summer we could easily have lost our crop, but thankfully we had weeks of warm, dry weather and so, whilst our grass had gone past its peak, it was still worth making into hay. One hot and sticky afternoon in late summer he began cutting. Three days later it was done.

I leaned on our gate and looked with quiet satisfaction at the bales dotted around the field, waiting for us to get hot and sweaty lugging them across the lane and into the barn. And that was when it happened. I felt it physically, like a warm glow deep inside, a fundamental shift somewhere in my consciousness and for a fleeting moment I felt a deeper connection to this land, to this village and to this life. It was the first tentative step on the journey of putting down roots, a long journey and one that couldn't be rushed. I hoped those roots would continue to grow but, knowing myself as I did, I suspected that there was a fine line between feeling grounded and feeling tethered. Time would tell which way the scales tipped.

Chapter 20

Jack Frost

❖ ❖ ❖

Winters tended to be mild and wet in our part of Wales but every now and then we'd get a rogue cold season which made smallholding life more testing. In our worst year temperatures dropped to minus ten at night and rarely rose above freezing during the day. Friends of ours who lived higher up in the hills were snowed in for three weeks. They had been through this before and solved the problem by leaving the car down in the village. The lane that led to their house was impassable, blocked by drifting snow that had set solid as the wind blew the bad weather across the hills, and so their only way out was a forty-five minute trek across the fields.

Our cottage was no more than a quarter of a mile from the main road but our lane had also frozen solid. If it had all been on the level we might have managed to get out, but the last section down to the pub was steep and lethal as it exited onto a busy road. We were cut off for at least a week which was made all the more irritating as we could see the cars driving to and fro down on the main road, so tantalisingly close, but we simply couldn't get to it. We had to cancel all the jobs we had booked in for that week and also lost a reservation for the B&B. Snowy weather may be pretty but it plays havoc with earning money.

It was a constant battle keeping the water for the animals from freezing solid, a fight we lost several times a day. It was so cold some mornings that the entire water bucket had turned to ice and even the hammer that now accompanied me on all my visits struggled to break it up. In a bid to make life easier I started taking an empty bucket down with me, along with a watering can filled up from the house, but that fresh bucket was often icing over again by lunchtime. We got through a mountain of hay and feed as the grass was buried deep. Snari, Bella and the sheep would paw at the snow, slowly working their way through to a tiny patch of frozen grass, even when they had a manger full of hay. Chickens don't have many facial expressions but there was no doubting how utterly fed up they were with the weather, bunched up and glaring at me as if it was my fault.

Getting dressed to go out became almost ridiculous with the number of clothes we put on: thermals, long-sleeved shirts, fleeces, thick coats, scarves and gloves. I waddled along the lane like a Michelin man (or woman), my movements clumsy, hampered by all the layers of clothing, my shoulders hunched up against the cold. Every trip outside felt like a battle and the weather was our enemy.

And yet it was beautiful. The gloom of winter was banished, erased overnight, and now our world was a bright white wonderland. The woods behind our cottage had been a band of dull browns and greys, bare branches clawing their way into a leaden sky. Now those branches were delicately coated with soft, fluffy snow, their outlines thrown into sharp relief against a blue sky. Ramshackle barns with half their roofs missing had been transformed from a derelict mess into a scene worthy of a Christmas card. Barbed wire fences were edged with ice crystals, sparkling like diamonds in the sunshine, and fence posts wore white hats. Even the sheep had succumbed to a winter makeover, a light dusting of snow landing on their coats as if someone had sprinkled them with icing sugar.

The snow turned Lucy and Maddie into puppies again: they threw themselves on their backs and rolled around in a frenzy, legs kicking and wriggling in all directions. They sank right down into the deeper snowdrifts, leaving us watching anxiously until they reappeared, biting and snapping at the snow as they clawed their way out, only to jump gleefully into the next one. We tried to walk up onto the hill behind us but it was incredibly hard work, less of a walk and more of a graceless stumble and tumble into snowdrifts that got deeper and deeper. Eventually we gave up and turned back for the warmth and safety of home. Beautiful as it was, one couldn't help but be aware that the mountains were dangerous places in winter.

The last couple of hundred yards before we reached home was down a drover's track, deeply pitted so you had to watch every step, with an unruly hedge-line arcing over our heads. Every now and then, I heard a crack and the loose snow crystals on the branches above would come loose and shower us in white crystals that slowly melted on our jackets. Looking up I could see no reason for this, no gust of wind or bird suddenly taking flight. In the deep silence that comes with a snowy landscape I had the fanciful notion that perhaps Jack Frost was up in the branches, mischievous and fey, following our progress, watching gleefully to see if we slipped and fell.

Jack Frost has been a fairytale character in songs and stories since the 1700s, harmlessly nipping at our noses in Christmas carols, but he has a darker side. Old fairy tales depict him as a capricious character with a low opinion of humans. Children were warned that it was dangerous to venture into the woods when the frost crackled in the branches, when an old man with a long white beard stood amongst the trees and the air could suddenly turn cold enough to freeze the breath from your body.

Back in modern-day Wales the light was fading, the air growing colder around us. Another branch deposited its load across my shoulders, sliding icy fingers down the back of my neck. I shivered and was glad we were only minutes away from home. Old Father Frost would have the woods to himself tonight.

Part 3

The letting go

Chapter 21

Transitions

❖ ❖ ❖

'Do you realise the freezer is still almost full?' I had taken out a frozen leg of lamb for our dinner that evening. 'If we have our usual number of lambs, we'll have to buy another freezer to put them in.'

'That would be daft,' said Michael. 'We could just sell more of them and not have any ourselves.'

'That doesn't feel right either.'

Later on that day I went back down to the garage, where we kept our meat freezer, and looked more specifically at the contents. Half of it was taken up by pork: bags and bags of sausages, enough to feed an army, even though we had only kept one pig for our own meat; a mountain of bacon, neatly split into packs of four rashers, and then there were the larger cuts, the chops, tenderloin, hocks, shoulders and belly. The pigs went months ago and we had hardly dented our store, despite using the sausages and the bacon for the B&B as well as for ourselves.

If one pig filled up half of the freezer it took several lambs to fill up the other half. I dug down to the bottom and looked at the dates. To my surprise and dismay I saw that a couple of the packs were well over a year old. I clicked the lid shut and went back indoors, deep in thought.

There had been no question of a freezer this full in our early years of smallholding. We were enthusiastic meat eaters and by the time we took the lambs to the abattoir the freezer was usually almost empty. I thought about our eating habits over the past year and realised that they had changed without me being fully aware of it. I tried to remember what meals we had cooked last week: some fish, chicken and pork, but at least three meals had been vegetarian. And when we did eat meat, we had smaller portions.

This shift in our eating habits had not been the result of some big life-changing decision. It had happened slowly and subtly. We simply found we enjoyed the taste of vegetables, particularly those that were home-grown, just as much as the meat, sometimes more so. I thought back to my childhood days with a wry smile. I had detested vegetables, to the point where I refused to eat them and had spent many a school lunchtime standing in the corner, banished there by an exasperated teacher for trying to hide my soggy cabbage under my potatoes so that it looked as if

I had made at least some effort to eat part of my lunch. You can take a horse to water, but you can't make it drink and my teacher – her face forever etched in my memory as she made my school days so miserable – never did succeed in making me eat my vegetables. If only she could see me now, tucking happily into vegetable lasagne, broccoli soup or lentil and sweet potato curry, not that such things were on the menu in my school days.

Part of the change in our diet may well have been as a result of a general greater public awareness that vegetables were good for you, a subconscious reaction to the 'five a day' advertising campaigns and the realisation that we all ate far more meat than our bodies needed for us to stay healthy. Growing our own vegetables had certainly made a difference, but I wondered if there was more to it than that. I remembered a comment from the lady we borrowed our first ram from. She'd said that she no longer took her lambs to market as she'd lost the appetite for it. Did she mean she no longer enjoyed eating the meat or no longer had the will to send her lambs to slaughter? Would there come a day when I felt the same way she did? I honestly didn't know. I still enjoyed meat and still felt strongly that our animals had the best lives that we could give them, but the annual visit to the abattoir was always a difficult day and didn't seem to get any easier with more experience.

Later that evening I pushed my plate away and breathed out a sigh of satisfaction.

'That was delicious.'

Michael nodded, still working his way through a second helping of roast lamb.

'What do you think about us having a break from lambing this year?' I asked.

'Why?'

'We don't need the meat. I figure we already have a year's supply in the freezer. It would be good to give the girls a rest year. And us as well. We could go camping instead of being tied down for the whole of the lambing season.'

And so it was agreed. And although I hardly acknowledged it, I knew that somewhere at the back of my mind I was glad I wouldn't be visiting the abattoir that year.

Unfortunately girls will be girls even if you take them away from the boys and so it didn't work out as we intended. I could hardly call my sheep girls really. In sheep years they were mature ladies but that didn't stop the hormones raging, particularly in Morag's case. Fate conspired against us as a farmer had a ram in an adjoining field and the combination of Morag flaunting herself like a wanton hussy and poor fencing meant that he got into our field. They had enough time together for her to get her wicked way with him before we descended upon them and put him back where he belonged. Luckily none of the other girls were impregnated, but it wouldn't be quite the lambing-free year that we had expected.

She gave birth to just one lamb, most unusual as she routinely had twins or triplets. He was a big lad and black as the night, not a speck of white on him, which was strange as his sire had been all white and Morag had the distinctive markings of a Jacob.

And it also meant that our freezer got topped up after all.

Chapter 22

Ladies that lunch

❖ ❖ ❖

'This is a rare treat,' said my friend Helen. 'We don't do this often enough.'

I nodded, my mouth full of halloumi and pomegranate seeds.

A new café had opened in our local town and we had decided to play at being 'ladies that lunch' and try it out. Neither of us had much time for this sort of thing, both of us too caught up in the responsibilities of running our respective lives. As self-employed people, financial security came from having fingers in many pies. Helen was a linguist with a translating and international tour-guiding business that she and her husband ran from home, and she also taught yoga classes in the evenings. Michael and I had our carpet cleaning and stone floor renovation business, as well as the B&B and the smallholding. On top of all this I somehow found the time to write two novels during those smallholding years, neither of them good enough to ever see the light of day. Free time, whatever that meant, was something of a luxury for both of us.

With the main course consumed with great satisfaction I decided I might as well make the most of the occasion and ordered a chocolate brownie that I really didn't have any room for while we discussed the sort of light, frothy subjects that you would expect from ladies who lunch, subjects such as the concept of time and how we manage it.

During my corporate marketing days out in the big wide world I had very little control over how I spent my time. I gained a salary and a good standard of living but, whilst it would be unfair to say I lost my soul, I certainly lost the feeling that I was in charge of how I spent my time or that life was fulfilling. When we took on our smallholding I had assumed that the pace of life would slow down and that I would have more time to call my own. It hadn't worked out that way, although with hindsight it was obvious to me that I had been hoping for something that was never going to happen. The smallholding was a new hobby, one that required a great deal of our time. We still needed to work and so adding the smallholding into the mix was always going to mean I had less free time, not more. If anything, it actually put pressure on us to earn more money, not less, so that we could afford the costs of keeping all our animals.

Running two businesses, with one of them being holiday accommodation, meant that there was rarely a week where we didn't have some sort of work commitment on a daily basis, including the weekends, and that was before we added in the responsibility of all our animals. Yet it felt completely different to those days of commuting to an office and staring at four walls all day. Nothing that I did felt like 'work' in the way that I had previously thought of the word. Instead of commuting around the M25, stuck in endless traffic jams, Michael and I drove to work through green lanes. Instead of sitting in tiny conference rooms, all white walls and fluorescent lighting, trying to look interested in presentations that seemed utterly pointless, my work was diverse and unpredictable: one day I could be stripping a stone floor in a grand country mansion, the next cleaning a carpet in a one-bed rented flat, and the people were as different as the houses in which they lived. Cringeworthy phrases like 'thinking outside of the box' disappeared from my vocabulary.

The animals were the best part of our lives. I found respite from the unrelenting busyness of each week by just being around them. When they weren't causing me angst and heartache by trying to die or be ill they gave me the greatest of all pleasures and a sense of inner peace and happiness that was only matched by spending time out in the magnificent landscape that surrounded us.

If how we use time can be measured by a tumbler and how

full of water it is, our tumbler was full to the brim. Every hour of every day was spoken for and if we ever found ourselves with a moment when nothing was happening we soon found a way to fill it. This is a perverse and particularly human trait which makes a nonsense of pursuing the holy grail of having more 'free' time. I had become so caught up in the pace of my life that I actually felt uneasy if I had an hour with no demands upon me. I wished I could take a lesson from the animals, who seemed to have a far more holistic approach to life, masters of living at a slow pace and perfectly content to do nothing else but just be. With so many commitments I was a little hamster on a treadmill of my own making and whilst I didn't mind, as long as it continued to make me happy and fulfilled, a treadmill is still a treadmill and needs a wary eye trained upon it. At the back of my mind was the niggling doubt that life shouldn't be this frenetic.

Perhaps it's all a question of perspective: the allure of the idea of free time is not necessarily that you have time to do nothing, but that it provides a space where each individual can choose how to spend that time in a way that is personally fulfilling, rather than having that decision foisted upon them by the demands of work and family.

'So have we decided that it's a good thing that we're this busy, or a bad thing?' asked Helen as we paused for breath.

'No idea. All I've done is confuse myself.' We smiled at each other happily, knowing we'd done the subject justice when we got to this point. A shadow fell across the table and a vaguely familiar male voice cut across our musings. It was a man I'd met briefly a few days ago whilst I was buying a bag of grain for the chickens at the local country store. He and his wife were visiting their holiday home and had popped in to get some dog food. The wife had struck up a conversation, saying how she had always wanted chickens and we had chatted for a while.

'Hello again,' he said. 'How's the good life going?'

I paused, not sure whether he wanted a one-word answer or a something more meaningful, but he carried on without waiting for a reply.

'My wife's still going on at me about getting out of London and buying a little place in the hills. Live a simple life. No worries. No responsibilities.' He shook himself, like a dog shaking off water. 'Can't say it's for me, probably rather dull I would imagine, but each to their own.'

Helen and I raised eyebrows at each other as he returned to his table and the wife who was never going to get her dream country cottage.

'I think the word "dull" must mean different things to different people,' I mused. 'And if he had to balance two jobs plus the marketing, finances and all the paperwork which paid for that good life, then he might not think it was quite so simple either.'

In fairness to the city dweller, the stereotypical idyll of 'a good life' naturally leads to the assumption that it would also be a simple one, the two fitting together like hand and glove. I had thought the same thing so I could hardly criticise others for taking the same view, but that version of myself had faded away long ago as time had shown me the truth of it. Two little words like good and simple could not begin to sum up the complexities and layers of this life.

Thankfully the waiter brought our bill over at that point and saved us from embarking upon a new discussion. Our precious interlude of free time, whatever that might mean, was over and now we would return to our day jobs. It would be many months before we found the time to meet again this way.

Chapter 23

Paradise lost part 1

❖ ❖ ❖

'What's wrong?' asked Michael, lifting his head from cleaning Snari's halter.

'Nothing,' I replied absently, staring out of the window. It was raining. It had been raining for what felt like forever.

'Yes there is. You're prowling about the place like you don't know what to do with yourself and you keep sighing.'

'Everything is fine. Apart from the weather.'

We fell back into silence. I leaned my chin on my hands and sighed.

'There!' exclaimed Michael triumphantly. 'You did it again. And it's nothing to do with the weather. We had some glorious days last week and you were still moping about.'

'It's nothing,' I repeated. 'Or maybe it's lots of little things.'

'Like what?'

'Maybe I feel that life is a bit stale at the moment, that's all. Our conversations are all about the animals. Or vegetables. Or if we want a really stimulating subject there's always the dilemma of rats in the compost bin. We live in Wales and we go on holiday in Wales. Not that we go on holiday much these days because of the animals. We grab a weekend here or there. It's been years since we've made it up to Scotland, let alone abroad. I can see our life mapped out ahead of us and we'll be having exactly the same conversations year in, year out until one of us dies.'

My words seemed to come out of my mouth of their own volition and took both of us by surprise.

'Oh,' said Michael. 'I didn't realise you were that unhappy.'

'I'm not unhappy. I don't know what I am. I just feel out of sorts. As if there should be more to life than this. Do you feel any of those things or is it just me?'

Now it was his turn to sigh. 'I know what you mean. I have days when I wish we weren't so tied down. But that's what a smallholding life is all about. It's a settled way of living, taking your pleasure from within that life, rather than from outside of it. I don't see that anything has changed, apart from how you feel about it.'

I nodded miserably. That was the problem. Our lifestyle hadn't changed but my perception of it had shifted. For a while it had been all I wanted but somewhere along the way I began to want something else. I couldn't pinpoint an exact time or a particular reason for this change, and I felt guilty for even thinking these thoughts, let alone saying them out loud, because I had no doubt that what we had was paradise. Or at least it had been. If I couldn't settle down and find contentment here then I had no idea what to do about it or what came next.

'I don't know how I feel about this being it for the rest of my life.' I said the words almost to myself. 'I don't know whether it will be enough.'

That's the thing with words. Once you've said them, you can't take them back. They're out there and, at some point, they will have to be dealt with. Part of me wished I'd kept the thought inside my head, but another part felt a sense of relief that I had finally acknowledged my feelings.

Michael and I looked at each other, our faces serious.

'What do we do with this?' he asked.

'I don't know.' I shrugged. 'Carry on as usual and hope that it's a phase and I'll come through it.'

'And what if you don't?'

I had no answer to give him. I had no idea where we would go from here. Neither of us wanted another house move, another major upheaval in our lives. We couldn't keep doing that. It wasn't the solution to the problem.

'Forget I even mentioned it,' I said briskly. 'It will pass. Maybe I just need a change of scenery. A proper holiday. And then I'll be fine.'

I hoped I sounded more convincing than I felt but from the worried look on Michael's face I knew he wasn't fooled. All we could do was wait, and hope that time would provide some answers.

Chapter 24

Making a difference

❖ ❖ ❖

The fire was dying out, the embers glowing a deep, demonic red. We had watched the summer sky fade from the blues of dusk to the black of the night, and conversation had slowly dropped away, leaving us free to do nothing more than watch the flames ebb and flow, comfortable together in the silence. Earlier in the day we had numbered twenty or more, squeezed into a small clearing in the woods where the land wasn't exactly flat but was sufficiently level to be able to cook and eat together. All those human bodies and noise had pushed the woodland away but now the trees reclaimed their territory, closing ranks around us, and shadows filled the empty spaces. There were only six of us left and it was time to think about finding a comfortable place to sleep, not an easy thing in a wood on a steep slope.

Earlier in the day I had perched on a tree stump, a plastic beaker of cider in one hand and a freshly barbecued sausage in a bread roll in the other, licking the tomato ketchup as it dripped through my fingers. I looked around at my companions. We were members of a local sustainability group and this was one of our projects. It was a community woodland that belonged to the village and we spent several days a month coppicing and clearing it, replanting certain areas and constantly repairing the fencing to keep the sheep on the adjoining farm from eating everything we planted. Today had been a social get-together, a time to eat and drink, relax and take stock of what we had done.

I hadn't known any of these people when I moved to the village but over the years they had become good friends. It had been a slow and satisfying process, the regular meeting at weekends as part of a group tipping over into invitations to each other's houses, conversations moving from everyday subjects to more personal revelations. We were mostly incomers, even though that included some people who had lived here for thirty years or more, and we shared common values and interests: a love and concern for nature and wildlife, the desire to live a sustainable lifestyle, a chilling sense of unease about what the human race as a whole was doing to both the planet and the climate. For those of us who were smallholders there was also the challenge of attaining some level of self-sufficiency as well as a commitment to animal welfare issues.

It sounds heavy stuff but we were just normal people with concerns, trying our best to do something about them. We couldn't claim to be perfect. Michael and I drove around in an old workhorse of a Land Rover, a practical choice although hardly good for the climate, but we tried to balance this by generating some of our power supply from solar panels, and from growing our own food or buying locally. The very fact that we humans exist is a problem. Unless someone wants to advocate a sudden mass extinction, all any of us can do is try to reduce our carbon footprint, to think about the consequences of our everyday actions and realise that the job will never be done, that there is always room for improvement.

Neither Michael nor I were activists or obvious rebels; we didn't go on marches or chain ourselves to railings. I've always been in awe of people who will push the boundaries to make changes, but I know I am not one of them. We can't all be heroes, not that everyone would use that term of course, but it's a free world and we all have the right to our own opinions, with the proviso that there are some lines which shouldn't be crossed. I recognised that my own form of protest, or action, was a much gentler one, to try and make a difference by living my life in a way that tried to uphold all those complex beliefs and concerns. I hoped that over time, the number of people who felt the same would grow and that fundamental changes in our society would come from the bottom upwards. It certainly didn't appear that our world leaders, politicians and the business world had any appetite for facing up to what was happening. The red flags of climate change were being raised by the likes of George Monbiot and James Lovelock but nobody in power did more than offer lip service in response. It spoke volumes that it took celebrities like Hugh Fearnley-Whittingstall and Jamie Oliver, chefs not politicians, to champion animal welfare issues and change the way people looked at the food they consumed.

Sitting there with my friends, I wondered how we would be regarded by the outside world. Would they see us as deluded tree-huggers or have a niggling feeling that our concerns were valid but there was nothing they could do and anyway it was enough of a struggle just to work and keep food on the table without worrying about the bigger picture? I had no doubt we were a minority but most of the time I had a sense of optimism and believed that we were a growing minority. There were other times when I didn't feel so hopeful, when it seemed that the human race was set on a course of destruction and heartache and our efforts were so inconsequential as to be almost pointless.

Were we making a difference? I wasn't too hopeful but only time would tell. Whatever happened it wouldn't change my feelings on the matter. There was a certain code by which I wanted to live my life, a standard to which I would hold myself accountable, regardless of what other people did. Our lives might change in the future, take twists and turns that we couldn't begin to foresee now, but I hoped that code would come with us, an integral part of who we were. If it all fell to pieces in the end, at least we could say we tried.

Chapter 25

Paradise lost part 2

❖ ❖ ❖

'Are we ready yet? Please tell me that you're done.'

Michael is the most patient of men but I could tell from his voice that he was reaching the end of the line. I avoided looking at him and went straight to the medicine cabinet and pulled out some purple antiseptic spray.

'Ellie is limping. It'll take me two minutes to put this on. Two minutes now will save us problems later on. I'll be really quick. I promise.'

This happened all the time. It was as if the animals instinctively knew when we were going out for dinner or away for a short break. The sheep were by far the worst culprits, and would store up all their problems until minutes before we were due to leave.

This time round our menagerie would have to get on with it by themselves. We were on our way up to Scotland for ten days, friends had offered to keep an eye on the animals, and I was determined to leave any niggling concern about the state of Ellie's feet behind me. We had a long, slow journey ahead of us as our old VW camper didn't like to go much above fifty miles per hour, and that was downhill with a following wind but, as the miles rolled slowly past, I could feel the ties loosening. By the time we reached the west coast of Scotland my mind had clicked into travelling mode.

The weather is even more of a lottery in Scotland than it is in Wales but we were lucky. We spent ten glorious days wild camping by lochs and in forests, exploring crumbling castles in hidden valleys and island-hopping on the west coast. It was perfect escapism, but you can never escape yourself, no matter how hard you try. We had come on this holiday because of that conversation a few months ago. This was the break that I hoped would put everything back into perspective, giving me a change of scenery and time to think, and hopefully afterwards I would slip back into our life at home and love it the way I had done before. The subject hadn't been discussed at all since that day, both of us actively skirting around any seemingly innocent topic that might lead us to it, and we didn't talk about it in Scotland either, but on the journey back there was a heaviness to our usually content silences and I wondered which of us would be the first to broach the subject.

'Well?' said Michael.

'Well what?' We had just left Fort William and were driving through Glencoe, magnificent and brooding, and part of me wanted to delay this conversation until we were out of Scotland, to hang on to the contentment of our trip for as long as possible.

'How do you feel about things now?' Michael persisted.

'How do *you* feel?'

'I asked first.'

I took a deep breath. 'The problem hasn't gone away. The reverse, if anything. I feel we are stuck in a rut, a wonderful rut admittedly, but it's not enough. I want more out of my life.'

That was the abridged version. Walking is a great way to clear the mind, to get to the heart of whatever might be vexing a person and these days of walking under clear Scottish skies had helped me to unravel my tangled emotions. Instead of continually trying to change myself, it was time to accept that I was a restless soul, to face it instead of running away from it. And yet, even as I said those words 'I want more' out loud, the doubting demon in my head whispered that I was being selfish and unrealistic. Why couldn't I settle for what was by most standards a very fulfilling life? What right did I have to demand more and to question everything we had built up together?

I turned and looked at Michael's profile, trying to get a hint of a reaction but there was nothing. I carried on.

'Whatever I want has to be tempered against what you want. If we're in different places on this then we think again.'

I waited.

'Are we in different places?' I could hear a note of desperation in my voice.

'Let's pull in for a coffee,' he said at last. 'I can't discuss this and drive.'

We came off the motorway at the next service station and found ourselves a quiet table in the corner. Now it was my turn to be silent and wait.

'I'm sort of with you,' he said. 'I can see that our life is full of routines and that they aren't going to change very much. The challenges and the big highs – and lows – of the early years are levelling out, so life isn't so exciting. But if we're seriously contemplating making a change there are huge implications. Both businesses are finally working well, giving us a good income. And then there are the animals.' He spread his hands and sighed. 'What are you saying? That we just walk away from it all on a whim?'

'We can't do this on a whim. It's a huge decision and we have to be sure it's right for us. But there are so many reasons to make a change. We're running ourselves ragged earning enough money to support our lifestyle and all the animals. If we simplified everything we'd need less money. We're doing all we can to save the planet, but we're paying a heavy personal price for it as our horizons have shrunk. This world is amazing, with so many places we've not seen, and I'm not ready to shut myself away in this valley for the rest of my life. It seems such a waste, as if we've got the balance wrong. It's about recognising that life is short and things can go wrong out of the blue. We're starting to lose friends and family to cancer, to illnesses that knock their lives off course and ruin all their dreams. It could happen to us at any time, and then it would be too late. At the moment we have good health and we're fit. This is our time to do something, not later.'

There are some conversations in all our lives which are pivotal, which turn everything on its head, and I could see from the way Michael was looking at me that this might be one of those moments.

'You say it's our time. To do what exactly?' he asked.

'Go travelling. The where and the how of it all we have to work out together. But I don't see why it should somehow be a sin to want the most out of life. We only get one life to live, why shouldn't we grab it with both hands and make it wonderful?'

'If we are going to do this it needs to be a clean break. And not just a few months travelling. A year or two at least.'

'Sounds great to me.'

And so it began. From that moment on we began to think outwards, rather than inwards. It was time to plan for a new future.

Chapter 26

Saying goodbye

❖ ❖ ❖

It was one of those days where spring is moving gently into the summer, when the air is soft and warm on the skin and there is nowhere else in the world that is as beautiful as Wales, or at least that was how I felt as I perched in my favourite place on the hillside above our valley. I remembered sitting here with Jessie, when Lucy was just a youngster, back in the early years of smallholding, looking down on our home, on our life, with a sense of wonder.

Things were different today. Jessie was dead and Lucy had taken her place as top dog, sitting beside me, a little closer than usual as if she knew something was happening. Maddie was scrummaging about in the undergrowth, oblivious to anything but her own world. I looked down on our home, on our life and knew that we would soon be leaving it. I loved this place with all my heart but if I stayed that love would turn sour and I couldn't bear the thought of turning these wonderful years, this precious time of our lives, into a bad memory. I wanted to remember it at its best, a love affair still fresh and exciting, rather than a marriage that had become stale and joyless.

I had measured our time here by the turning of the seasons, four of them every year, familiar and reassuring, but each of us have our own seasons within our lifetimes, unpredictable patterns of movement where we try a new life, perhaps a different job, a different country, a new partner or lifestyle. There are so many reasons that people move on, always with a sense of the unknown, a risk as to whether it will prove to be a good decision, or a bad one. We had spent months talking through our options since that holiday up in Scotland, looking for the negatives as well as the positives, trying not to allow ourselves to be too easily seduced by the thought of a new start. All our discussions led us to the conclusion that this was the right thing for us to do.

We had put our cottage up for sale six months ago and had been lucky to find a buyer quickly, one who knew the area and wanted the property enough to offer the full asking price. Our plan was to take a couple of years out travelling. Europe was on the doorstep and we had planned a circular road trip that would include many countries we didn't know: from the northern countries of Norway, Sweden and Finland, on through the Baltic states of Estonia, Latvia, Lithuania, and then into Poland, Slovakia, Hungary, Croatia and Slovenia before heading home via a more familiar route through Italy, France and Spain to Portugal. We had amassed a veritable library of travel books to help us navigate our way through all these countries, including a second-hand collection of Rough Guides or Lonely Planet for each of them. The timing was perfect as we had a long summer ahead of us. There was no getting away from the fact that our carbon footprint would increase but we felt we had built up some credits over the last eight years. It was a compromise, as almost any form of travel is, but we could live with it.

We had budgeted a certain amount from the house sale to fund our trip and when the money ran out then we would come back and look for a property with some land in Wales and start up a small eco-friendly camping and glamping business.

We were due to exchange on the house sale today. It had been a fraught process, not helped by a long chain, but the estate agent had confirmed yesterday that the last outstanding mortgage offer was through. Everybody was finally ready. Both of us were on edge, waiting for the call, and as a watched phone never rings I had taken myself and the dogs out for a walk to try and calm my nerves. Completion had been pencilled in for two weeks' time and everything was in place, ready to be actioned once we got this call. We had a buyer interested in the carpet cleaning equipment, with the possibility of taking on the business as a going concern, but that was yet to be confirmed. Space had been reserved at a container storage business on a nearby farm where we could put all the house contents until we returned and we had booked a big transit van as we would be physically moving ourselves. The couple who were buying our house were keen to take on the B&B business so we had continued to take bookings on their behalf. We had sold our camper van and bought a second-hand Hymer motorhome, more suitable for full-time travelling.

Deciding what to do with the animals had been the hardest decision. Some good friends with a smallholding on the other side of the valley had bought all the sheep from us and had kindly taken the chickens as well. I knew they would be well looked after, and perhaps even have a better life as they would have access to the open hillside, with much more space to roam than we had been able to give them. I would be able to see them when we came back to visit but even so I felt quite tearful as we loaded them into the trailer. When we let them out the other end and they saw the open land in front of them, they left me without a backwards glance.

Bella went back to her previous owner, another wrench as she would be one of a large number of animals and probably wouldn't have as much personal attention as we had given her. The pigs weren't an issue as they had only ever been with us for short stretches of time and, once we knew we were leaving, we hadn't got any more.

We took the most time over finding a home for Snari, putting an advert on the website of the Icelandic Horse Society of Great Britain. He had a number of health issues and, at the age of twenty-three, was no longer a youngster, although the Icelandic breed is a long-lived one so he could reach forty years old. Because of his health problems we didn't want any money for him, but he had to go to someone who would really love him. Five people came to see him, all women, all seemingly genuine people so it was hard to choose. When Michael had first bought Snari there were a few tricky months where he would bolt whilst riding out in the hills, galloping off out of control and very hard to bring back, and it took a long time for him to trust Michael enough to work through that. As each of these women rode him, people he didn't know, I could see that he was becoming nervous and edgy. This was of concern because if they had problems with him they would either want to return him to us, impossible as we would not be there, or would then sell him on. We wanted to know he had a secure future, as far as that is ever possible in the world of buying and selling horses.

One particular woman handled him far better than any of others. I could see him tensing as she mounted him, see him pulling at the bit, and I tensed with him, hoping he wouldn't race off with her. She was calm, firm and relaxed, aware that he was on edge but not worried by it. He relaxed with her, his ears came forward and he moved off happily. Michael and I exchanged a glance and we both knew this was the right one.

The dogs would be coming with us. They loved travelling, associating it with walking all day long and being able to sleep underneath our bed so life would only get better for them with this lifestyle change. We were as ready as we could be but it had been a huge undertaking to get to this point and both of us were drained by the process.

I headed back to the house. I could hear the phone ringing as I walked in through the gate and sprinted up the steps. Michael arrived from the other end of the garden just as I picked up the phone, both of us breathing hard. It was the estate agent. The person at the bottom of the chain had got cold feet and pulled out right at the very last minute. He was going to buy somewhere in Greece instead. The whole thing had collapsed.

Bad news can be hard to comprehend, particularly if your whole life hangs upon it. To begin with there was a complete sense of disbelief that this had happened at all, that we could get to this stage without a solicitor or estate agent, somewhere down the chain, being aware that there had been a problem. As the reality began to sink in we had a time of pointless anger and after that we slid into depression. We didn't know what to do with ourselves. Everything that had made this place our home was gone. I would walk down into the village and see an empty field where my sheep had been, would stand on the patch where we kept the chickens, usually full of fluffy little bodies scratching away at the earth, clucking at each other, running over to peck at my feet, and hear only silence. Michael would prowl aimlessly round the house in the morning, no pigs, no Snari, no Bella, no-one to look after. Saying goodbye to our animals had been so very hard, and it had all been for nothing.

From being manically busy, completely focused on our move, now we had time on our hands. Too much time. We had been winding the business down and now had to decide what we should do, start it up again or hope we found a new buyer quickly and wait it out. None of the choices open to us seemed good ones.

In the end, the person at the bottom of the chain quickly found a new buyer, and with the rest of the chain still miraculously intact, the process began again. A seller halfway down the chain decided that in the intervening months prices had gone up and so she increased her selling price by £15,000, a take-it-or-leave-it ultimatum. That increase worked its way up to us, each buyer and seller negotiating a compromise to keep the deal alive. We were at the top of the chain with no-one to pass the increase on to, and the result was that we had to drop our price by £8,000 or start again. It was a big chunk of money and would eat into the funds we had earmarked for travelling but we had no choice.

Three months later we completed. By this time it was September and not such a good time to begin a European tour.

As the memory of the recent disaster was still raw we had developed a sceptical attitude towards things happening when they were supposed to and so had not made any firm plans about what we would do when, or if, we finally completed. We had booked ourselves in at a nearby campsite in the Brecon Beacons and would decide what we were going to do from there.

The morning of the move had been chaotic. We had been working until midnight to clear away the last of our things and up again at six am, frantically throwing things in the van without any thought other than to be out of the way when the new owners arrived. We were late and they were late, so we crossed paths briefly with the removal men, fractious at having to manoeuvre their pantechnicon up such a narrow lane. When they realised they had to fit the contents of a four-bedroomed house into our little two-bedroomed cottage, through low doorways and an impossible staircase, they looked quite desperate. We fled the scene, feeling sorry for all of them.

We had only a short journey to our campsite, squeezing Hillie, our motorhome, through lanes that became ever narrower, until we found ourselves alone in a field with a standpipe for a fresh water supply and a manhole cover for waste. This suited us perfectly. It was as close to wild camping as you could get. We were less than twenty miles from what had been home, but it felt so different that it could have been a thousand miles away.

Freedom is just a word, seven letters, and yet it is one of the most powerful, beguiling and emotive words in not just the English language but in any language. *La liberté* in French, *die Freiheit* in German, *eleftheria* in Greek and *rhyddid* in Welsh. In Russian it's pronounced *svah-boh-dah,* in China *zìyóu,* in Hebrew it's *Hofesh.* No matter where you were born in this world, this is one of those rare words that unites everyone, a word everyone understands. In some places it is taken for granted, in others it is a dream, a way of life that people long for. I stood beside our ancient Hymer van, our home for the foreseeable future, or at least for the next few years which is as far into the future as I can ever go, and felt free. Utterly, wonderfully free.

Free from responsibilities, from possessions and clutter, from a daily routine, from worrying about money, from worrying about anything. Free from juggling all the balls that made up my life, constantly making decisions, constantly making lists so that I didn't forget anything. Now the only decisions we needed to make would be where to stop for the night and what to eat.

All these years later I can vividly picture myself standing in that field, can recall how sweet it felt, can still sense that physical lightening of a load that I hadn't fully realised was quite so heavy until it was lifted from my shoulders. There was another facet to our new-found freedom that I hadn't expected and that was freedom from ourselves. We were no longer defined by what we did: carpet cleaners, accommodation providers or smallholders. As of this moment we could recreate ourselves, become explorers, nomads, free spirits. In this new life no-one would know who we had been, would have no expectations of us and could only take us as they found us.

It really was a new beginning in the fullest sense of the word and I shall never forget how it felt.

Chapter 27

How did that *happen?*

❖ ❖ ❖

I look back on what happened next and struggle to explain it to myself. We took one look at our wonderful, amazing new life and then turned our back on it.

We decided to delay our European tour until spring of the following year. We wanted to see the countries we would be travelling through when they looked their best, warm and sunny, with leaves on the trees and blue skies, when we could eat outside on long summer evenings. More of the campsites and tourist attractions would be open and we would have the whole season to begin our long journey south. This year we would remain in Wales, not exactly renowned for its balmy winter weather, but it would give us an opportunity both for a period of prolonged hillwalking and also to explore potential areas that might be suitable for our future camping business. Many campsites in Wales closed over the winter, but enough remained open for it to be a workable idea.

The dogs thought this new regime was wonderful, each walk welcomed as if it was their last, come rain or shine and, despite the fact that there was a great deal more rain than shine, we also welcomed the long days of doing nothing more than putting one foot in front of the other, of immersing ourselves in the beauty of the hills and falling deeply, contentedly asleep each night, allowing our minds to empty, to learn the new, simple patterns of each day. As we moved leisurely around the country we noted each area for its potential as a future home and business. We didn't expect to find anything this soon, but even if we did, it wouldn't change our plans. We would buy it and then lock it up and leave it. Just walk away. It would still be there when we came back. We were leaving in April 2013 and nothing was going to get in our way.

Then we found something.

It was a seventeenth-century stone-built cottage set in the hills between Aberdyfi and Dolgellau in north Wales. Standing in the small garden on a clear, sunny day, the wide sweep of Cardigan Bay was a dazzling sight. The lane ended at the cottage, as this was the last, and the highest, inhabited dwelling on the hill. From the front door a spider's web of tracks led around the coastline and also inland, one walk offering a particularly tempting option of a fifteen-mile trek through the wilderness to Cader Idris with hardly any evidence to prove that mankind existed: no roads, no houses, nothing but sheep and skylarks for company. It was a walker's paradise. It was a nature lover's dream.

We had put together a list of 'must have' features for our new project, obvious things like flat land, a sheltered position suitable for a campsite, and easy access. From our own point of view we wanted a small house that needed very little work doing on it. This cottage didn't tick one single box on that list, in fact it put a big black cross in every one of them. It was totally unsuitable and yet still we bought it, testament to how easy it is to see only what you want to see.

We persuaded ourselves that we had room to squeeze a shepherd's hut in the far corner of the garden and to turn the dilapidated barn into a letting room, an alternative idea to camping, but one that would still bring in an income. The cottage was charming, the current owners consummate homemakers, the place so cosy that I wanted to sit by their fire with a cup of tea and never leave. It had solid stone walls two feet thick with a woodburner for heat and whilst there were areas that might need a bit of work, it didn't look too daunting.

It could so easily not have happened. If one were to believe in parallel universes there were countless points along the timeline where we could have chosen a different path. The estate agent that fateful day had shown us a property that didn't appeal at all and just happened to mention that she had another property that had recently come on the market, so recent that she hadn't even had time to prepare the details yet. We weren't really interested but she drove us up there on the way back to her office and the moment we saw it we were lost.

After several visits the rose-tinted glasses had dimmed enough for us to see that there was more work to be done than we had first realised and so we put in a ridiculously low offer. This could have been another point when we would have taken a different path as we never expected the vendors to accept it, but they did.

We took possession on December 23rd, hiring yet another van and carting all our furniture up from the storage yard back down near Crickhowell over several trips. We spent Christmas Day in the chaotic euphoria of the newly-moved-in, trying to cook a chicken in an inherited, ancient oven where the door wouldn't shut. Boxing Day saw the oven out on the drive, a harbinger of what was to come.

In January we left for an eight-week trip around Asia, backpacking around Thailand, Cambodia and Laos as if we were still teenagers. April rolled around, but instead of leaving for our grand European trip we stayed put, initially entranced by the incredible location but then becoming increasingly enmeshed in the process of what turned out to be a massive renovation project.

The shackles were back on, all our plans and schemes for a carefree life on the road blown away in the wind.

What happened to our dreams of becoming explorers and adventurers? What happened to the people who were supposed to be sitting at a pavement café in the warm Italian sunshine with a map spread out on the table, planning the next step of their journey? How could our commitment to that new life have been so weak, so easily derailed?

I can't answer those questions, even now. I can only think that we weren't as ready as we thought we were for that new life, weren't yet brave enough to take a chance and so instead we settled for four years of endless DIY. Each small job turned into a big job and we were consumed by it.

As the years went by we learnt that this location, idyllic when the weather was kind, could be challenging when the elements turned savage and that winters lasted a long, long time. We were at an altitude that put us in the cloud line, spending too many days lost in the mist. On so many occasions I would walk the dogs ten minutes down the hill and find myself in bright sunshine. I dreaded walking back up into that wall of fog, struggled to breathe in the clammy air. The wind was a regular companion, blasting in from the Irish Sea, whipping across Cardigan Bay, straight up the valley below us. In one particularly bad storm, the wind speeds gusted around 100 mph. I stood in our entrance hall, watching in horror as the tree roots of the huge conifer at the entrance to our drive lifted beneath the gravel, contorting like massive worms straining to reach the surface, as the tree rocked under the onslaught. When I couldn't bear to watch any more I went and stood in the conservatory, where I could see the corrugated panel roof of the old barn, weighted down by ropes and stones as a temporary measure to keep it in place, lifting a foot in the air at one end and then banging back down, again and again. I had my hands pressed against the windows and could literally feel them bending inwards with the pressure. It was not a place for camping, or even for a shepherd's hut. It wasn't a place I wanted to be.

It was a difficult time in our lives, a time of mixed blessings. There was no doubting the magnificence of the natural world around us: long sandy beaches, estuaries flanked by heather-clad hills, hidden ravines and waterfalls, the harsh splendour of the mountains. To come and visit such unspoilt, sparsely populated places is one thing; to try and earn a living in them is another. We resurrected our carpet cleaning business but with such a small population the income it brought in was a fraction of what we used to earn further south. In a bid to solve our growing concern about how we would earn our living I trained to be a Pilates instructor and ran classes in the surrounding village halls. This was another one of those times when fate nudges you in a direction you never expected to go. My back problems had returned with a vengeance and so I had looked for Pilates classes to see if they could ease the pain. As this part of Wales was still several years behind the rest of the country in keeping up with the latest exercise trends, there were none to be found, so I bought a book and taught myself. That book changed my life. I became a convert and decided I wanted to teach Pilates, to help other people as it had helped me.

I also studied for a diploma with the London School of Journalism and began to submit travel articles to various magazines. I had spent years writing fiction as a hobby, always consigning each half-finished novel to the bottom drawer in disgust, and was surprised to learn that I preferred non-fiction and, even better, that I could earn money from doing so. In the future it would lead me into writing books about our lives and our travels.

As we couldn't afford to employ the army of builders and tradesmen that would be needed to renovate the cottage, Michael became a jack-of-all-trades so that we could get the job done. He learnt how to strip a roof, replace all the timbers and retile it. He put in a new kitchen and a bathroom, rebuilt the stairs, and even mastered the art of plastering, an impressive feat as it is one of the hardest of all the building trades.

Whenever it all got too much, we escaped in Hillie, for short breaks in the mountains or further up the coast, and abroad when we could afford it. When we got back home I would write articles about our travels: Switzerland on a shoestring, winter in Spain and Portugal, cycling around Bruges, island-hopping around Scotland, on the cider trail in Wales, and a series of articles on gardens around the UK. I wrote campsite reviews, motorhome reviews, fillers about anything that seemed interesting. As the months went by I developed a relationship with a couple of magazine editors and the work came in more steadily.

As we were travelling so much I applied to the Caravan Club to see if they wanted any campsite inspectors and struck gold. Due to expected changes in regulations with Brexit they had to reassess the European campsites that they marketed in their brochures and were recruiting a team of health and safety inspectors for a one-off blitz. We were in the right place at the right time and we joined the team despite having no experience in health and safety issues. We spent two months inspecting campsites in France, Austria, Switzerland, Croatia and Hungary. We had so many sites to visit, and such large distances to travel, that it proved to be a punishing schedule, but it was a key piece of the puzzle that was moving us in a different direction.

By the time we got to the end of that summer, three years after we had moved to north Wales, we were different people. Each time we left home, it became harder to come back. The house felt like a millstone around our necks and we knew that finally we were ready to move on. We'd had to go through this blip, this diversion from our original plans, in order to come out the other side. Perhaps it proved that you get to where you need to be eventually but, whatever the reason, we had no regrets.

In these intervening years our dream had changed. Taking a few years out to travel and then coming back to buy another house and start up yet another business no longer appealed to us. We could see more clearly now that we would find ourselves right back at square one in a few years' time, restless and ready to move on again. It was time to stop trying to change ourselves, stop trying to force the proverbial round peg into a square hole, and accept that we had terminal wanderlust. This time round it really did need to be a clean break.

We decided to do something completely different. We decided we would buy a boat.

This idea was not quite as mad as it might sound. Michael had spent many years at sea. The type and size of boat we were thinking of buying would be much smaller than what he had been used to, but he was at ease on the water, in his natural element, which was just as well as I was not. Many centuries ago, in my student days, I had joined a sailing club, pottering about on small dinghies in a filled-in gravel pit. I enjoyed it when I was the crew, but tended to capsize the boat as soon as I took control of the tiller.

Michael had a hankering to buy a yacht and sail off into the sunset, but that was before he realised how dangerous I was on anything with sails. Instead we decided we would buy a motor cruiser, using the money from the sale of the house to buy us a boat big enough to live on comfortably, while we explored the canals and rivers of Europe. It seemed the perfect solution: we could travel as much as we pleased, stop whenever we wanted to, be it for a week or a winter, and when the wanderlust struck again, as it surely would, all we had to do was slip the lines and we would be on the move again. No more house purchases, no more fraught house sales. We could live a truly nomadic existence, and our home would come with us.

A quick look at the cost of the type of boat that we were looking for confirmed that it would cost less than the money we would realise from the house sale. We would put the bulk of that money in savings, set aside enough for us to cruise for two years, and then decide about how to supplement our income after that.

We put the house on the market, vowing fervently that this really was the last time we were going to put ourselves through this, and began to search for a boat.

Mary-Jane Houlton

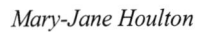

Part 4

Moving on

Chapter 28

Finding 'Olivia Rose'

❖ ❖ ❖

There are an astonishing number of boats for sale, both in Europe and in the UK. In no time at all we had looked at over a hundred of them, many online, some through visiting boatyards in France and Belgium, and whilst some had been tempting, none of them had felt quite right. We had never intended to buy a boat in the UK as it meant we would have to get it across the Channel, but when we saw the advert for this particular boat it seemed to fit so many of our requirements that we had to go and see it, which explains how we came to visit a riverside community on the River Trent, not far from Nottingham. Each plot housed a private mooring, some with no more than a wooden jetty, others with an additional small cabin or quirky dwelling, raised up on stilts as the Trent was prone to flooding. An eclectic selection of boats large and small spread out along the river on either side of this mooring but we had eyes for only one of them, *Olivia Rose*.

She was a Dutch motor cruiser, thirteen metres long and three and a half metres wide, small enough to feel like a proper boat rather than a house that happened to be on the water, but big enough to be comfortable for living on. Her hull was painted navy blue, her upper decks white and, despite being twenty-six years old, she was immaculate. I looked at her and felt something pull at my heartstrings. It wasn't just that she was a beautiful boat, it was more that she felt like home to me from the moment I first saw her.

I have never fully understood the human compulsion to feel a strong connection to inanimate objects. However this lack of understanding has never stopped me from getting sentimental about lumps of metal and unreliable engines, hence the fact that we had names for both our old VW camper and our motorhome and it was a sad day when we sold them.

Lester and Katy, the couple who owned the boat, had lived aboard her full time for nine years. She had originally been named *Frances Rose* but they had changed the name to *Olivia Rose*, after Lester's daughter. They were selling her to follow their own dream of early retirement and buying a catamaran to sail around the Greek islands. It soon became obvious that saying goodbye to her was going to be very hard for them.

Many boats are used only in the summer months, but

because she had been a proper full-time home for them, *Olivia Rose* was unusually well kitted out: a warm wooden interior, a well-appointed galley kitchen with full size oven, fridge, hob, washing machine, a woodburner and an additional central heating system powered from the same diesel tanks that ran the engine, a decent shower and toilet, a walk-around bed, loads of storage space, seating in the galley and the wheelhouse, the former folding down to offer a guest bed, and both an indoor and an outdoor driving position. Everything was spotlessly clean and, from what we could see, in good condition.

Boats are complicated creatures, being a combination of a house and a vehicle, so the conversation encompassed not just the mechanics of the central heating system but also discussions about the size of the engine, the state of the bilges, and the thickness of the hull. At some point I reached information overload. I sat down on a bench in the wheelhouse, letting the technical details waft over my head, and watched the river flowing gently past. There is something soothing about constant motion, a similar feeling to that of sitting in front of an open fire, watching the flames flicker, falling and rising, endlessly reinventing themselves. The far bank was cloaked in its spring finery, and as I watched a duck swam out from under the dense mat of branches resting just above the waterline.

'I spend ages sitting here.' Katy had come to join me. 'There's always something to watch.'

'Aren't you going to miss this?' I asked.

'Very much,' she replied. 'But it's time for a change. I just hope we won't regret it.'

Later on they took us out on the river so we could put *Olivia* through her paces. I watched Michael as he took the wheel for the first time and could see how at ease he was, as if he belonged there. My reaction was different, for this was all so strange to me. Up until now, this new adventure of ours had been in the future tense, but I knew that today we had found our boat and suddenly it was real, immediate. I took a turn at the helm, feeling the way she responded as the wheel spun through my fingers, and knew that the relationship with this particular inanimate object was going to put all the others into the shade.

'We don't get to take her out much these days,' explained Lester. 'There's only so many times you can go up and down the same stretch of river. Boats should be on the move, not stationary, so it would be nice to think she would go to someone who was going to cruise in her.'

We moored up again, thanked them for all their time, and said we would be in touch. That evening we made them an offer and they accepted.

That was the exciting bit, similar to when you find your dream home and your offer is accepted. Then comes the sobering reality of getting through the mountain of paperwork and legal procedures that leads you to finally taking possession of the keys.

Our first job was to organise and pay for surveys, both internal and external, which meant she had to be lifted out of the water. Lester moved her to a marina with hardstanding facilities in Newark so that the surveyor could check out the hull thicknesses. Ultrasonic readings were taken at three-foot intervals all over the hull and the keel and she was pronounced sound. The bow thruster was in good working order, the bilges free of any leaks; escape hatches, davits and cleats were all in good condition. There were a few minor things to deal with internally, which Lester sorted out for us. The first major hurdle had been cleared.

The insurance company had a list of requirements they needed satisfying and there were legal requirements for owning and cruising a boat in the UK as well as the European countries we would be passing through. Michael, as skipper, needed an International Certificate for the Operation of Pleasure Craft, and a short-range VHF Radio Certificate. Luckily he already had both of these from his seafaring days. He also had to take a CEVNI (Code Européen des Voies de Navigation Intérieure) test, which gave him a certificate to say he was aware of the European Waterways regulations. As the one and only crew member, there was no official requirement for me to have similar qualifications, but I had resolved that I would get them at some point in the future, just so that I knew what I was doing. In the meantime, Michael would teach me all that he knew.

'I'm looking forward to this,' he crowed. 'As crew, you have to do what the skipper says. Insubordination will not be tolerated.'

Olivia also had some paperwork hoops to jump through. (We thought her full name suited her very well but it was a bit of a mouthful so we shortened it to *Olivia* when we spoke of her.) We had to get all the fire extinguishers tested by the local fire brigade, which earnt us another certificate for our ever-growing boat file, and we had to update the Small Ships Register so that it had our name on it as the new owners. And lastly, we purchased a *vignette*, a licence which permits you to use the French waterways. It cost just over 400 euros for a year and a copy had to be fixed to the window in the wheelhouse so that the lock-keepers could see it.

Whilst we were preparing for our new life on the water, we were simultaneously working through the process of selling the house in Wales. It felt odd, as if our spirits had moved on already and were with *Olivia* but our bodies remained tethered to bricks and mortar. We had found a buyer and hoped to complete in April, which would give us plenty of time to cruise along the Trent, down the coast, across the Channel and into France. May came and went, but the house sale dragged on. By the time June came around everybody was getting twitchy. It should have been a relatively simple sale, but old properties such as ours have covenants to be negotiated and our buyer's mortgage provider and solicitor went through the usual game of avoiding all communication and blaming each other for each successive delay. Lester and Katy stuck with us, although they must at times have thought they had made a big mistake. By July patience on all sides was running out. The boat sale was at risk and we were contemplating putting the house back on the market and then at last the wheels turned and the sale was completed in early August. We bundled all our belongings into yet another storage container and walked away. If this all worked out for us, we would have to come back and sell the contents, but if it didn't, at least we still had a chair to sit on and a bed to sleep in.

That first weekend on board was a busy one. We were lucky in that we could park our van right next to our mooring, which made moving in easier. It took longer than it should have as we kept stopping for tea breaks so we could sit up on deck, look around the marina, watch the ducks and keep an eye out for the resident kingfisher. Then it seemed churlish not to chat to passing boat owners, and cast a critical eye on how well they handled their boats as they cruised out of the marina, the latter primarily done by Michael as I would only know they'd done it badly if they actually hit something. The fact that this was our boat and our life still didn't feel real. It was wonderful, but it felt like a new pair of walking boots that hadn't been properly worn in yet, shiny ones without any scuff marks. It would take time before they felt like old friends and fitted as snugly as the old pair had done.

Chapter 29

What now?

❖ ❖ ❖

'So what do we do now?' Michael raised the question that had been on both our minds.

The relief in finally owning *Olivia* was intense but the long delay in the sale of the house had implications for our cruising plans. We had lost the summer and now had to decide whether to spend the winter on *Olivia* in England, which didn't appeal, or risk the unpredictable weather of autumn on the long trip down the east coast and across the Channel.

'Suppose the weather is bad at Ramsgate and we can't cross over?' I asked.

'We have to wait it out. But the mooring costs there are very high. It's not a good place to be stuck. Plus I'm not sure about the engine.'

'What do you mean?' I stared at him. 'It's a bit late to say that now after we've bought her.'

'There's nothing obviously wrong at all. She seems to be running well from what I can tell. But it wasn't a new engine when they put it in the boat. It was already fourteen years old, a weird thing to do really, even though it had been fully reconditioned. Plus she's spent most of the last nine years just sitting at her moorings, and that isn't good for an engine. The Channel is one of the busiest waterways in the world and not a place for a boat that you're unsure about. If things went wrong it could be a disaster.'

We decided instead to put her on a trailer and take her across on a P&O ferry which would at least give us a few months cruising in France before the winter set in. Given what lay ahead, this cautious approach turned out to be one of our better decisions.

We got in touch with a haulage company who specialised in moving boats between Europe and the UK and were lucky in that they had already scheduled a trip across to France to pick up a boat that had terminal engine problems. It was limping its way slowly up to the north of France, in search of a suitable marina where it could be craned out. Sharing the transport costs meant we got a good deal and so a few weeks later we spent the day watching our boat swinging gently in a cradle as a crane lifted her out of the water and deposited her onto the biggest trailer I had ever seen. We followed the lorry in convoy and I had to keep pinching myself to check that I was awake and not lost in a daydream. At no point in my previous life had I ever foreseen a day when I would be driving round the M25 following my boat on its way to Dover. It was surreal.

We stayed at an Airbnb that night, ready for an early morning ferry crossing the next day. On August 23rd 2017, a momentous day in our lives if ever there was one, *Olivia Rose* was driven off the ferry into France. Within minutes we found the road blocked due to roadworks.

'Marvellous,' I muttered anxiously, watching closely to see what Ben, the driver of our lorry, would do now. 'Looks like he's following the diversion signs. Not got much choice I guess.'

The diversion took us round the backstreets. Our respect for Ben grew with each moment that passed as this diversion was never meant for a vehicle this size. At times he had to mount the pavement to get through, inching past lamp posts and road signs with millimetres to spare. Eventually, with everything still in one piece, we arrived at the launching ramp at the Grand Large marina at Dunkirk.

The crane picked *Olivia* up, with Michael on board, and set her gently down in the water. I scampered along to the far side of the marina to the berth that we had been allotted and took the ropes as he drove her in. We had made it! I'm sure the occasion should have been marked with a bottle of very expensive bubbly, but we still had one final loose end to tie up. From now on our only methods of transport would be by the boat, our bikes and on our feet. We hadn't been able to find a storage facility in France for the van, but there was one back in Dover and so, once we had unloaded the last few items from the camper van, including the dogs, Michael turned tail, and got back on the afternoon ferry to drop the van off. He would stay the night in Dover and come over as a foot passenger the following morning.

Being on *Olivia* in a tidal marina felt very different to those first two weeks we had spent on the River Trent, which had been a calm, tranquil experience by comparison. The tidal range was between three to six metres so twice a day all the boats, and the floating pontoons they were attached to, rose and fell with the tide. The boat rocked continuously, not helped by the wind getting up, or by the wash of passing boats as this was a busy marina. I had never been on a boat in this situation before and didn't feel entirely at ease with it. It got worse as I lay in bed alone that night, the fenders thudding against the hull in the wind every time I was on the point of falling asleep and the ropes screeching as *Olivia* shifted restlessly on the water. Over the coming months I would become familiar with these various noises, but that first night it felt very alien and I didn't sleep well.

I breathed a sigh of relief when the morning came and I could occupy myself with two important jobs so that we could get on our way once Michael returned. The first thing was to find the man who could fill up our diesel tanks for us. We had two tanks on board, with a combined capacity of 500 litres. Given that they were now almost empty it was going to cost a fortune to fill up. The second thing was to find out what the procedure was for getting through the nearby sea-lock and onto the inland waterways network.

I sat on deck eating my morning cereal, watching cormorants landing on the navigational posts outside the marina, spreading their wings out to dry in the warm sea breeze. Seagulls squabbled over mussels, dropping them onto the concrete wharfs from up on high to try and break the shells. The marina had berths for 250 boats, most of them occupied by yachts, so I was surrounded by a sea of masts, the halyards constantly tinkling, with only a few motor cruisers for company. This was also an industrial port, with cranes breaking up the skyline and tugboats continually coming and going. Everywhere I looked there was a sense of movement, of purpose. A huge seagoing ship inched majestically into the Trystram sea-lock on the far side of the marina and I felt a knot of apprehension in my stomach at the thought of sharing that lock with one or more of them the next day. That feeling in my stomach was going to become a familiar companion over the next few months – I had a steep learning curve ahead of me. I had absolute faith in Michael as my skipper, but it didn't change the fact that every single aspect of this new life of ours would be a personal challenge for me, something completely different and where I would have no expertise, and no knowledge of how things worked. This was not an easy situation for a self-confessed control freak who liked to know what was coming and who had Plan A mapped out to the finest detail, and Plan B in reserve. Part of me was fine with this, because I needed to push the boundaries every now and then, but the flip side of feeling challenged and exhilarated is feeling nervous, maybe even terrified at times. I didn't know how well I would react to these unknown situations ahead and part of me was scared that I would be found wanting.

Pushing these unhelpful thoughts firmly aside I called the dogs for a walk ashore so they could relieve themselves. They weren't happy about this new mooring; it was far too lively for them and a far cry from our mooring on the river, where they had easily been able to hop off onto a grassy bank. In protest they had been spending most of their time lying under the table, subjecting me to 'why have you done this to us?' looks, to which I had no good answer. Lucy had never been at ease in water and would have a panic attack the minute she got out of her depth. Both of them had to be coaxed on and off the boat. Pontoons are unstable, wobbly things, not suitable for dogs born and bred in the solidity of the Welsh hills. I had to lift them down, one at a time, and then half drag them along the length of a larger, slightly more solid pontoon that led to the walkway up onto terra firma. This walkway, like the whole marina, also moved with the tide and so at times it was a steep pull up and down. The dogs' claws had nothing to purchase on and I felt guilty for putting them through this but a dog goes where its owner goes and there's nothing to be done about it. The whole process had to be repeated on the way back but something went wrong as Lucy took a panicky leap from the pontoon up onto the boat before I could lift her on. She slid off backwards into the water, which wouldn't have been so bad but she was sandwiched between the pontoon and the boat moored up next to us. She went right under, disappeared from view for a few heart-stopping seconds when I feared she had gone under the other boat, and then resurfaced, thrashing about wildly, completely beside herself.

My hand shot out of its own volition and I grabbed her by the neck. A Dutch man on a nearby yacht ran to my aid and between us we pulled her out. With her fur completely soaked through to the skin, she seemed a much smaller, vulnerable version of herself. She had a good shake, soaking both me and her Dutch rescuer, and grudgingly accepted a rigorous towelling down, but once safely reinstalled in her safe space under the table in the galley, seemed none the worse for wear. I, on the other hand, was a complete wreck, having nearly lost my dog before we'd even gone anywhere. I suspected her ageing hips had let her down, or possibly she had simply slipped, but either way we were going to have to keep a close eye on her.

The Turning of the Seasons

Chapter 30

The adventure begins

❖ ❖ ❖

Olivia's skipper returned later that day, to a joyous reception from both the crew and the dogs. The next morning we slipped the lines and cruised out of the marina and through the Trystram sea-lock, which turned out to be far less intimidating than I had expected. An hour later we had left the tidal waters behind and were motoring gently down the Canal de Bourbourg, one of the network of short canals outside Dunkirk.

We motored for six hours that first day, covering thirty-eight kilometres. There was something wonderfully reassuring about being on a body of water where you can see the banks on either side and where the water level stays broadly the same. It was a perfect day, blue skies and sunshine, with only four locks to pass through and time to watch the world drift slowly by. We were heading for Arques, a small port on the Canal l'Aa, for our first night and as we arrived I looked at our mooring options with an anxious eye, wondering how Lucy would cope. I needn't have worried. There was space alongside and a grassy bank for easy access.

Later that evening we sat up on deck and watched the sun go down.

'So what did my crew make of her first day?' Michael asked.

'Well, my ropes got in a muddle in every single lock. I can't imagine ever driving her into a lock myself without crashing into the gates. But other than those small details, it was a good day. In fact it was a very good day.'

We fell back into an easy silence and I thought how those few words didn't begin to sum up what I felt. After today this life finally felt real. After today I had a feeling in my heart that I was where I was meant to be, pursuing a way of living where I could belong, where I hoped I could be content, where the simple fact that we were always moving would allow me to settle, a paradox which might seem contradictory but made absolute sense to me. I've always believed that if anybody chased a dream for long enough, they would eventually catch up with it, but I know it's not a given. Life holds no guarantees and this opportunity was precious, to be valued and protected.

As the sun fell the temperature dropped. It was the last weekend in August and autumn was around the corner. Michael had turned fifty this year, and I was fifty-seven. If you look at a lifetime in terms of seasons, we were in the autumn of our lives and it seemed fitting that our personal timeline had dovetailed with autumn in the natural world as we began our journey. If we still lived in the time of Greek gods and myths, I am sure this coincidence would be seen as a good omen. Those superstitious times are long gone, but I held onto that thought.

From here we would travel where the water took us, with *Olivia* as our guide and our companion. France would be our starting point, with Luxembourg, Germany, Belgium, the Netherlands and even further afield waiting to be explored in the future. If we liked a particular spot, we could stop for a while, but if not we would just keep moving. Slow travel, where the journey mattered more than the destination. There would be ups and downs, problems to face, testing times as well as good ones because this wasn't a journey to escape life, rather to find a way of living it differently.

Would this be a change that would see us through the rest of our lives or would we be looking for something else with heavy hearts in a couple of years? Only time would tell, but as we set off the next morning I knew it would be worth it, no matter how long it lasted.

The Turning of the Seasons

❖ ❖ ❖

Please review this book!

If you have enjoyed reading *The Turning of the Seasons*, I would be so grateful if you could leave a review on Amazon. If you'd rather not do a written review you can easily leave a completely anonymous star rating. These personal reviews and ratings are what sell books so they really matter.

Acknowledgements

As always a big thank you to my publishing team, Louise Lubke Cuss at WordBlink for copy editing, Georgia Laval at Laval Editing for formatting and the team at Ebook Launch for the cover design. This is the third book we have produced together and I feel incredibly fortunate to have such a talented and professional group of people working with me. Thanks also to my beta readers, Helen Isaacs, Tricia Houlton, Vanessa Couchman and Eliza Waters – your insights and comments have made this a better book. I am very grateful to Trisha Loncraine for her shared insights on life as a hill farmer, and this book is written with loving memories of her husband Tony, much loved and never forgotten. My husband Michael has provided the wonderful drawings. Writing a book is an emotional journey, one where Michael is always at my side, giving encouragement and having faith in me when confidence reaches a low ebb. And last, but by no means least, a huge thank you to you, my readers, for your support in buying the books and your encouragement through the lovely reviews that you leave. I couldn't do this without you.

About the author

Mary-Jane is a travel writer who has travelled extensively throughout Europe. She has a Diploma in Freelance Journalism and Travel Writing from the London School of Journalism and has had numerous features published in a variety of magazines, but it is sharing her experiences through writing books that gives her the most pleasure.

Just Passing Through: A nomadic life afloat in France, her first book, is part memoir, part travelogue. It gives an account of the life she and her husband Michael lead on board their boat *Olivia Rose* as they travel through the rivers and canals of France.

Due to the pandemic and the consequences of Brexit, further cruising plans were temporarily put on hold and life went off at an unexpected tangent. In the autumn of 2020 Mary-Jane and Michael found themselves living in an off-grid cabin with five acres of field and woodland near the Pyrenees in France. Out of this was born her second book, *A Simple Life: Living off-grid in a wooden cabin in France*, which explores how it feels to live in a tiny home with no electricity, no kitchen, no bathroom and where the loo is a bucket in a shed.

The Turning of the Seasons: Tales of a smallholding life is her third book and takes us back to a more settled time in their lives, before they began their nomadic adventure afloat. Now that the world is hopefully getting back to some semblance of normality, although a very fragile one, *Olivia Rose* is back on the water once more and Mary-Jane is busy writing her fourth book.

You can follow or contact Mary-Jane on her weekly blog at https://theoliviarosediaries.com.

Excerpt from *Just Passing Through*

If you have started with this book, then you might like to read the next chronological book in the series, *Just Passing Through – A nomadic life afloat in France.*

Less is more

There is something irresistibly romantic about the idea of living on a boat. It suggests a life of freedom, of open skies and sun on your face, a simpler yet richer existence.

In 2016, my husband Michael and I made the decision to sell our house, rid ourselves of all our possessions, close down our business and buy a motor cruiser to explore the inland waterways of Europe. We did this because we were looking for a different way of living. After decades of trying to establish roots and settle down, we finally accepted that we were nomadic by nature, forever restless, always needing to know what was around the next corner. We had also realised that the modern-day treadmill of earn-more-to-buy-more made no sense to us. We had never been materialistic but now we found we wanted even less, not more.

This book is a record of our travels, but I hope it also gives an insight into how it feels when you walk out of a secure and comfortable life and into another, very different one. We soon learnt that everything changes when you live on the water. Some days are filled with wonder, whilst others can be frustrating and challenging. On deck our horizon expanded, but inside the boat our living space contracted – there is an art to living in small spaces with few possessions. Relationships, not just with each other, but also with the friends and family we left behind, would need to be strong to survive the demands of this type of life. Some passed the test, others did not. On a personal level, when faced with so much that was unknown and which, at times, took me far out of my comfort zone, I came to know myself better. I am not sure if this life changed me, or simply brought something that had always been there, buried deep within me, to the surface.

I hope you enjoy our adventures as much as we have. Should any reader be tempted to follow in our footsteps, I have included an information section at the end of the book with practical advice to help you on your way.

Chapter 1 – Going for a song

'Do you think anyone will come?' I looked anxiously up at the sky. The clouds were that particular shade of grey that we do so well in winter in the UK, leaching the colour out of everything, and the wind was picking up.

Michael shrugged. 'We'll soon find out.'

It was the middle of January in North Wales and we were holding a yard sale. Not just any old yard sale. We'd sold our house six months ago in order to buy a boat. We'd bundled all our worldly goods into storage in our rush to get onto the water in France before the winter. That had only ever been a short-term solution, and today was the day of reckoning.

The sum total of the last fourteen years of our lives together lay sprawled around the storage container yard. The furniture from a four-bedroom cottage; a huge collection of tools which we'd amassed over the years as we renovated our home and which we knew would go for a fraction of what they were worth; pictures, rugs and ornaments, curtains, garden pots and countless personal items that were worth nothing to anybody else but held years of memories for us.

Some items were harder to part with than others. Michael's face took on the expression of a grieving relative each time he walked past his precious sea kayak. I ran sad, apologetic fingers over a book collection that went back to my childhood. It felt as if we were selling off old friends.

There is nothing that will keep the great British public from the prospect of grabbing a bargain, and so I needn't have worried about the weather. They burst in through the gates as if this was the last yard sale they would ever see, jostling for prime position and the chance to be the first to find that priceless heirloom that we might have overlooked. We were short on heirlooms, but it didn't seem to matter. They riffled through boxes, peered eagerly inside wardrobes, fingered the fabrics and fiddled with electrical goods. They haggled down, we haggled up and the pile of our possessions slowly disappeared.

Two of our friends turned up to help and surveyed the scene with a look of mounting panic on their faces.

'What can we do?' they asked, as I looked helplessly at the sea of faces in front of me and tried to remember if I'd really said it was only a fiver for my favourite wool rug.

'Pile in anywhere you like.' I nodded towards the table stacked high with the contents of the kitchen. 'That would be a good place to start.'

'Is it all priced up?'

'Nope. We tried but gave up. Too many things. Just do the best you can.'

It was a crazy day. There was no time for a cup of coffee, for lunch, even to go to the loo, let alone time to feel sad or peeved at things we had worked so hard to buy disappearing for mere pennies. If anything, there was a sense of elation as the day wore on and we realised that we were going to sell the lot.

By four pm the yard was empty save for a van from the local reclamation yard. He had offered us a deal to take anything that was left. We heaved an old wardrobe up, squeezed in the last of the cardboard boxes beside it and let out a sigh of relief as it spluttered its way out of the gates. Suddenly it was quiet.

'I need a beer,' said Michael.

We took over a table in the corner of the local pub and counted up piles of notes and coins around our drinks and packets of crisps. It came to just over £2,000. We looked at each other, unsure whether to laugh or cry. It was a poor price for all the things that had made our house a home, but then I guess that much of what we'd owned was more shabby than chic. We knew we could have got a better return if we'd sold the quality items individually over the internet but we didn't have the time, or a base from which to do it.

On the other hand, £2,000 bought us another six weeks of time on the water, which was how we now measured the value of money. We had achieved what we set out to do today, which was to rid ourselves of the last ties from our previous life.

It was done. We were free.

Printed in Great Britain
by Amazon